M000291403

Cygwin User Guide

A catalogue record for this book is available from the Hong Kong Public Libraries.

Published in Hong Kong by Samurai Media Limited.

Email: info@samuraimedia.org

ISBN 978-988-8406-23-4

Background Cover Image by https://www.flickr.com/people/webtreatsetc/

Contents

Abstract

Cygwin User's Guide

Chapter 1

Cygwin Overview

1.1   What is it?

Cygwin is a Linux-like environment for Windows. It consists of a DLL (cygwin1.dll), which acts as an emulation layer providing substantial POSIX (Portable Operating System Interface) system call functionality, and a collection of tools, which provide a Linux look and feel. The Cygwin DLL works with all x86 and AMD64 versions of Windows NT since Windows XP SP3. The API follows the Single Unix Specification as much as possible, and then Linux practice. The major differences between Cygwin and Linux is the C library (newlib instead of glibc).

With Cygwin installed, users have access to many standard UNIX utilities. They can be used from one of the provided shells such as **bash** or from the Windows Command Prompt. Additionally, programmers may write Win32 console or GUI applications that make use of the standard Microsoft Win32 API and/or the Cygwin API. As a result, it is possible to easily port many significant UNIX programs without the need for extensive changes to the source code. This includes configuring and building most of the available GNU software (including the development tools included with the Cygwin distribution).

1.2   Quick Start Guide for those more experienced with Windows

If you are new to the world of UNIX, you may find it difficult to understand at first. This guide is not meant to be comprehensive, so we recommend that you use the many available Internet resources to become acquainted with UNIX basics (search for "UNIX basics" or "UNIX tutorial").

To install a basic Cygwin environment, run the **setup.exe** program and click Next at each page. The default settings are correct for most users. If you want to know more about what each option means, see Section 2.1. Use **setup.exe** any time you want to update or install a Cygwin package. If you are installing Cygwin for a specific purpose, use it to install the tools that you need. For example, if you want to compile C++ programs, you need the gcc-g++ package and probably a text editor like nano. When running **setup.exe**, clicking on categories and packages in the package installation screen will provide you with the ability to control what is installed or updated.

After installation, you can find Cygwin-specific documentation in the /usr/share/doc/Cygwin/ directory.

Developers coming from a Windows background will be able to write console or GUI executables that rely on the Microsoft Win32 API instead of Cygwin using the mingw32 or mingw64 cross-compiler toolchains. The **-shared** option to GCC allows to write Windows Dynamically Linked Libraries (DLLs). The resource compiler **windres** is also provided.

1.3   Quick Start Guide for those more experienced with UNIX

If you are an experienced UNIX user who misses a powerful command-line environment, you will enjoy Cygwin. Developers coming from a UNIX background will find a set of utilities they are already comfortable using, including a working UNIX shell. The compiler tools are the standard GNU compilers most people will have previously used under UNIX, only ported to the

Windows host. Programmers wishing to port UNIX software to Windows NT will find that the Cygwin library provides an easy way to port many UNIX packages, with only minimal source code changes.

Note that there are some workarounds that cause Cygwin to behave differently than most UNIX-like operating systems; these are described in more detail in Section 3.9.

Use the graphical command **setup.exe** any time you want to update or install a Cygwin package. This program must be run manually every time you want to check for updated packages since Cygwin does not currently include a mechanism for automatically detecting package updates.

By default, **setup.exe** only installs a minimal subset of packages. Add any other packages by clicking on the + next to the Category name and selecting the package from the displayed list. You may search for specfic tools by using the Setup Package Search at the Cygwin web site.

After installation, you can find Cygwin-specific documentation in the `/usr/share/doc/Cygwin/` directory.

For more information about what each option in **setup.exe** means, see Section 2.1.

1.4   Are the Cygwin tools free software?

Yes. Parts are GNU software (**gcc**, **gas**, **ld**, etc.), parts are covered by the standard X11 license, some of it is public domain, some of it was written by Red Hat and placed under the GNU General Public License (GPL). None of it is shareware. You don't have to pay anyone to use it but you should be sure to read the copyright section of the FAQ for more information on how the GNU GPL may affect your use of these tools. If you intend to port a proprietary application using the Cygwin library, you may want the Cygwin proprietary-use license. For more information about the proprietary-use license, please go to http://www.redhat.com/services/custom/cygwin/. Customers of the native Win32 GNUPro should feel free to submit bug reports and ask questions through Red Hat channels. All other questions should be sent to the project mailing list cygwin@cygwin.com.

1.5   A brief history of the Cygwin project

Note

A historical look into the first years of Cygwin development is Geoffrey J. Noer's 1998 paper, "Cygwin32: A Free Win32 Porting Layer for UNIX® Applications" which can be found at the 2nd USENIX Windows NT Symposium Online Proceedings.

Cygwin began development in 1995 at Cygnus Solutions (now part of Red Hat, Inc.). The first thing done was to enhance the development tools (**gcc**, **gdb**, **gas**, etc.) so that they could generate and interpret Win32 native object files. The next task was to port the tools to Win NT/9x. We could have done this by rewriting large portions of the source to work within the context of the Win32 API. But this would have meant spending a huge amount of time on each and every tool. Instead, we took a substantially different approach by writing a shared library (the Cygwin DLL) that adds the necessary UNIX-like functionality missing from the Win32 API (`fork`, `spawn`, `signals`, `select`, `sockets`, etc.). We call this new interface the Cygwin API. Once written, it was possible to build working Win32 tools using UNIX-hosted cross-compilers, linking against this library.

From this point, we pursued the goal of producing Windows-hosted tools capable of rebuilding themselves under Windows 9x and NT (this is often called self-hosting). Since neither OS ships with standard UNIX user tools (fileutils, textutils, bash, etc...), we had to get the GNU equivalents working with the Cygwin API. Many of these tools were previously only built natively so we had to modify their configure scripts to be compatible with cross-compilation. Other than the configuration changes, very few source-level changes had to be made since Cygwin provided a UNIX-like API. Running bash with the development tools and user tools in place, Windows 9x and NT looked like a flavor of UNIX from the perspective of the GNU configure mechanism. Self hosting was achieved as of the beta 17.1 release in October 1996.

The entire Cygwin toolset was available as a monolithic install. In April 2000, the project announced a New Cygwin Net Release which provided the native non-Cygwin Win32 program **setup.exe** to install and upgrade each package separately. Since then, the Cygwin DLL and **setup.exe** have seen continuous development.

The biggest major improvement in this development is the 1.7 release in 2009, which dropped Windows 95/98/Me support in favor of using Windows NT features more extensively. It adds a lot of new features like case-sensitive filenames, NFS interoperability, IPv6 support and much more.

The latest big improvement is the 64 bit Cygwin DLL which allows to run natively on AMD64 Windows machines. The first release available in a 64 bit version is 1.7.19.

1.6 Highlights of Cygwin Functionality

1.6.1 Introduction

When a binary linked against the library is executed, the Cygwin DLL is loaded into the application's text segment. Because we are trying to emulate a UNIX kernel which needs access to all processes running under it, the first Cygwin DLL to run creates shared memory areas and global synchronization objects that other processes using separate instances of the DLL can access. This is used to keep track of open file descriptors and to assist fork and exec, among other purposes. Every process also has a per_process structure that contains information such as process id, user id, signal masks, and other similar process-specific information.

The DLL is implemented as a standard DLL in the Win32 subsystem. Under the hood it's using the Win32 API, as well as the native NT API, where appropriate.

Note
Some restrictions apply for calls to the Win32 API. For details, see Section 2.2.2, as well as Section 3.1.8.

The native NT API is used mainly for speed, as well as to access NT capabilities which are useful to implement certain POSIX features, but are hidden to the Win32 API.

Due to some restrictions in Windows, it's not always possible to strictly adhere to existing UNIX standards like POSIX.1. Fortunately these are mostly corner cases.

Note that many of the things that Cygwin does to provide POSIX compatibility do not mesh well with the native Windows API. If you mix POSIX calls with Windows calls in your program it is possible that you will see uneven results. In particular, Cygwin signals will not work with Windows functions which block and Windows functions which accept filenames may be confused by Cygwin's support for long filenames.

1.6.2 Permissions and Security

Windows NT includes a sophisticated security model based on Access Control Lists (ACLs). Cygwin maps Win32 file ownership and permissions to ACLs by default, on file systems supporting them (usually NTFS). Solaris style ACLs and accompanying function calls are also supported. The chmod call maps UNIX-style permissions back to the Win32 equivalents. Because many programs expect to be able to find the /etc/passwd and /etc/group files, we provide utilities that can be used to construct them from the user and group information provided by the operating system.

Users with Administrator rights are permitted to chown files. With version 1.1.3 Cygwin introduced a mechanism for setting real and effective UIDs. This is described in Section 3.6. As of version 1.5.13, the Cygwin developers are not aware of any feature in the Cygwin DLL that would allow users to gain privileges or to access objects to which they have no rights under Windows. However there is no guarantee that Cygwin is as secure as the Windows it runs on. Cygwin processes share some variables and are thus easier targets of denial of service type of attacks.

1.6.3 File Access

Cygwin supports both POSIX- and Win32-style paths, using either forward or back slashes as the directory delimiter. Paths coming into the DLL are translated from POSIX to native NT as needed. From the application perspective, the file system is a POSIX-compliant one. The implementation details are safely hidden in the Cygwin DLL. UNC pathnames (starting with two slashes) are supported for network paths.

Since version 1.7.0, the layout of this POSIX view of the Windows file system space is stored in the /etc/fstab file. Actually, there is a system-wide /etc/fstab file as well as a user-specific fstab file /etc/fstab.d/${USER}.

At startup the DLL has to find out where it can find the /etc/fstab file. The mechanism used for this is simple. First it retrieves it's own path, for instance C:\Cygwin\bin\cygwin1.dll. From there it deduces that the root path is C:\Cygwin. So it looks for the fstab file in C:\Cygwin\etc\fstab. The layout of this file is very similar to the layout of the fstab file on Linux. Just instead of block devices, the mount points point to Win32 paths. An installation with **setup.exe** installs a fstab file by default, which can easily be changed using the editor of your choice.

The fstab file allows mounting arbitrary Win32 paths into the POSIX file system space. A special case is the so-called cygdrive prefix. It's the path under which every available drive in the system is mounted under its drive letter. The default value is /cygdrive, so you can access the drives as /cygdrive/c, /cygdrive/d, etc... The cygdrive prefix can be set to some other value (/mnt for instance) in the fstab file(s).

The library exports several Cygwin-specific functions that can be used by external programs to convert a path or path list from Win32 to POSIX or vice versa. Shell scripts and Makefiles cannot call these functions directly. Instead, they can do the same path translations by executing the **cygpath** utility program that we provide with Cygwin.

Win32 applications handle filenames in a case preserving, but case insensitive manner. Cygwin supports case sensitivity on file systems supporting that. Since Windows XP, the OS only supports case sensitivity when a specific registry value is changed. Therefore, case sensitivity is not usually the default.

Cygwin supports creating and reading symbolic links, even on Windows filesystems and OS versions which don't support them. See Section 3.1.6 for details.

Hard links are fully supported on NTFS and NFS file systems. On FAT and other file systems which don't support hardlinks, the call returns with an error, just like on other POSIX systems.

On file systems which don't support unique persistent file IDs (FAT, older Samba shares) the inode number for a file is calculated by hashing its full Win32 path. The inode number generated by the stat call always matches the one returned in d_ino of the dirent structure. It is worth noting that the number produced by this method is not guaranteed to be unique. However, we have not found this to be a significant problem because of the low probability of generating a duplicate inode number.

Cygwin 1.7 and later supports Extended Attributes (EAs) via the linux-specific function calls getxattr, setxattr, listxattr, and removexattr. All EAs on Samba or NTFS are treated as user EAs, so, if the name of an EA is "foo" from the Windows perspective, it's transformed into "user.foo" within Cygwin. This allows Linux-compatible EA operations and keeps tools like **attr**, or **setfattr** happy.

chroot is supported since Cygwin 1.1.3. However, chroot is not a concept known by Windows. This implies some serious restrictions. First of all, the chroot call isn't a privileged call. Any user may call it. Second, the chroot environment isn't safe against native windows processes. Given that, chroot in Cygwin is only a hack which pretends security where there is none. For that reason the usage of chroot is discouraged.

1.6.4   Text Mode vs. Binary Mode

It is often important that files created by native Windows applications be interoperable with Cygwin applications. For example, a file created by a native Windows text editor should be readable by a Cygwin application, and vice versa.

Unfortunately, UNIX and Win32 have different end-of-line conventions in text files. A UNIX text file will have a single newline character (LF) whereas a Win32 text file will instead use a two character sequence (CR+LF). Consequently, the two character sequence must be translated on the fly by Cygwin into a single character newline when reading in text mode.

This solution addresses the newline interoperability concern at the expense of violating the POSIX requirement that text and binary mode be identical. Consequently, processes that attempt to lseek through text files can no longer rely on the number of bytes read to be an accurate indicator of position within the file. For this reason, Cygwin allows you to choose the mode in which a file is read in several ways.

1.6.5   ANSI C Library

We chose to include Red Hat's own existing ANSI C library "newlib" as part of the library, rather than write all of the lib C and math calls from scratch. Newlib is a BSD-derived ANSI C library, previously only used by cross-compilers for embedded systems development. Other functions, which are not supported by newlib have been added to the Cygwin sources using BSD implementations as much as possible.

The reuse of existing free implementations of such things as the glob, regexp, and getopt libraries saved us considerable effort. In addition, Cygwin uses Doug Lea's free malloc implementation that successfully balances speed and compactness. The library accesses the malloc calls via an exported function pointer. This makes it possible for a Cygwin process to provide its own malloc if it so desires.

1.6.6 Process Creation

The `fork` call in Cygwin is particularly interesting because it does not map well on top of the Win32 API. This makes it very difficult to implement correctly. Currently, the Cygwin fork is a non-copy-on-write implementation similar to what was present in early flavors of UNIX.

The first thing that happens when a parent process forks a child process is that the parent initializes a space in the Cygwin process table for the child. It then creates a suspended child process using the Win32 CreateProcess call. Next, the parent process calls setjmp to save its own context and sets a pointer to this in a Cygwin shared memory area (shared among all Cygwin tasks). It then fills in the child's .data and .bss sections by copying from its own address space into the suspended child's address space. After the child's address space is initialized, the child is run while the parent waits on a mutex. The child discovers it has been forked and longjumps using the saved jump buffer. The child then sets the mutex the parent is waiting on and blocks on another mutex. This is the signal for the parent to copy its stack and heap into the child, after which it releases the mutex the child is waiting on and returns from the fork call. Finally, the child wakes from blocking on the last mutex, recreates any memory-mapped areas passed to it via the shared area, and returns from fork itself.

While we have some ideas as to how to speed up our fork implementation by reducing the number of context switches between the parent and child process, fork will almost certainly always be inefficient under Win32. Fortunately, in most circumstances the spawn family of calls provided by Cygwin can be substituted for a fork/exec pair with only a little effort. These calls map cleanly on top of the Win32 API. As a result, they are much more efficient. Changing the compiler's driver program to call spawn instead of fork was a trivial change and increased compilation speeds by twenty to thirty percent in our tests.

However, spawn and exec present their own set of difficulties. Because there is no way to do an actual exec under Win32, Cygwin has to invent its own Process IDs (PIDs). As a result, when a process performs multiple exec calls, there will be multiple Windows PIDs associated with a single Cygwin PID. In some cases, stubs of each of these Win32 processes may linger, waiting for their exec'd Cygwin process to exit.

1.6.6.1 Problems with process creation

The semantics of `fork` require that a forked child process have *exactly* the same address space layout as its parent. However, Windows provides no native support for cloning address space between processes and several features actively undermine a reliable `fork` implementation. Three issues are especially prevalent:

- DLL base address collisions. Unlike *nix shared libraries, which use "position-independent code", Windows shared libraries assume a fixed base address. Whenever the hard-wired address ranges of two DLLs collide (which occurs quite often), the Windows loader must "rebase" one of them to a different address. However, it may not resolve collisions consistently, and may rebase a different dll and/or move it to a different address every time. Cygwin can usually compensate for this effect when it involves libraries opened dynamically, but collisions among statically-linked dlls (dependencies known at compile time) are resolved before `cygwin1.dll` initializes and cannot be fixed afterward. This problem can only be solved by removing the base address conflicts which cause the problem, usually using the `rebaseall` tool.

- Address space layout randomization (ASLR). Starting with Vista, Windows implements ASLR, which means that thread stacks, heap, memory-mapped files, and statically-linked dlls are placed at different (random) locations in each process. This behaviour interferes with a proper `fork`, and if an unmovable object (process heap or system dll) ends up at the wrong location, Cygwin can do nothing to compensate (though it will retry a few times automatically).

- DLL injection by BLODA. Badly-behaved applications which inject dlls into other processes often manage to clobber important sections of the child's address space, leading to base address collisions which rebasing cannot fix. The only way to resolve this problem is to remove (usually uninstall) the offending app. See Section 3.5.1 for the `detect_bloda` option, which may be able to identify the BLODA.

In summary, current Windows implementations make it impossible to implement a perfectly reliable fork, and occasional fork failures are inevitable.

1.6.7 Signals

When a Cygwin process starts, the library starts a secondary thread for use in signal handling. This thread waits for Windows events used to pass signals to the process. When a process notices it has a signal, it scans its signal bitmask and handles the signal in the appropriate fashion.

Several complications in the implementation arise from the fact that the signal handler operates in the same address space as the executing program. The immediate consequence is that Cygwin system functions are interruptible unless special care is taken to avoid this. We go to some lengths to prevent the sig_send function that sends signals from being interrupted. In the case of a process sending a signal to another process, we place a mutex around sig_send such that sig_send will not be interrupted until it has completely finished sending the signal.

In the case of a process sending itself a signal, we use a separate semaphore/event pair instead of the mutex. sig_send starts by resetting the event and incrementing the semaphore that flags the signal handler to process the signal. After the signal is processed, the signal handler signals the event that it is done. This process keeps intraprocess signals synchronous, as required by POSIX.

Most standard UNIX signals are provided. Job control works as expected in shells that support it.

1.6.8 Sockets

Socket-related calls in Cygwin basically call the functions by the same name in Winsock, Microsoft's implementation of Berkeley sockets, but with lots of tweaks. All sockets are non-blocking under the hood to allow to interrupt blocking calls by POSIX signals. Additional bookkeeping is necessary to implement correct socket sharing POSIX semantics and especially for the select call. Some socket-related functions are not implemented at all in Winsock, as, for example, socketpair. Starting with Windows Vista, Microsoft removed the legacy calls `rcmd(3)`, `rexec(3)` and `rresvport(3)`. Recent versions of Cygwin now implement all these calls internally.

An especially troublesome feature of Winsock is that it must be initialized before the first socket function is called. As a result, Cygwin has to perform this initialization on the fly, as soon as the first socket-related function is called by the application. In order to support sockets across fork calls, child processes initialize Winsock if any inherited file descriptor is a socket.

AF_UNIX (AF_LOCAL) sockets are not available in Winsock. They are implemented in Cygwin by using local AF_INET sockets instead. This is completely transparent to the application. Cygwin's implementation also supports the getpeereid BSD extension. However, Cygwin does not yet support descriptor passing.

IPv6 is supported beginning with Cygwin release 1.7.0. This support is dependent, however, on the availability of the Windows IPv6 stack. The IPv6 stack was "experimental", i.e. not feature complete in Windows 2003 and earlier. Full IPv6 support became available starting with Windows Vista and Windows Server 2008. Cygwin does not depend on the underlying OS for the (newly implemented) `getaddrinfo` and `getnameinfo` functions. Cygwin 1.7.0 adds replacement functions which implement the full functionality for IPv4.

1.6.9 Select

The UNIX `select` function is another call that does not map cleanly on top of the Win32 API. Much to our dismay, we discovered that the Win32 select in Winsock only worked on socket handles. Our implementation allows select to function normally when given different types of file descriptors (sockets, pipes, handles, and a custom /dev/windows Windows messages pseudo-device).

Upon entry into the select function, the first operation is to sort the file descriptors into the different types. There are then two cases to consider. The simple case is when at least one file descriptor is a type that is always known to be ready (such as a disk file). In that case, select returns immediately as soon as it has polled each of the other types to see if they are ready. The more complex case involves waiting for socket or pipe file descriptors to be ready. This is accomplished by the main thread suspending itself, after starting one thread for each type of file descriptor present. Each thread polls the file descriptors of its respective type with the appropriate Win32 API call. As soon as a thread identifies a ready descriptor, that thread signals the main thread to wake up. This case is now the same as the first one since we know at least one descriptor is ready. So select returns, after polling all of the file descriptors one last time.

1.7 What's new and what changed in Cygwin

1.7.1 What's new and what changed in 2.4

- New, unified implementation of POSIX permission and ACL handling. The new ACLs now store the POSIX ACL MASK/-CLASS_OBJ permission mask, and they allow to inherit the S_ISGID bit. ACL inheritance now really works as desired, in a limited, but theoretically equivalent fashion even for non-Cygwin processes.

  To accommodate standard Windows ACLs, the POSIX permissions of the owner and all other users in the ACL are computed using the Windows AuthZ API. This may slow down the computation of POSIX permissions noticably in some circumstances, but is generally more correct. The new code also ignores SYSTEM and Administrators group permissions when computing the MASK/CLASS_OBJ permission mask on old ACLs, and it doesn't deny access to SYSTEM and Administrators group based on the value of MASK/CLASS_OBJ when creating the new ACLs.

  The new code now handles the S_ISGID bit on directories as on Linux: Setting S_ISGID on a directory causes new files and subdirs created within to inherit its group, rather than the primary group of the user who created the file. This only works for files and directories created by Cygwin processes.

- cygpath has a new -U option, which creates cygdrive paths using the unambiguous /proc/cygdrive prefix.

- New API: rpmatch.

- Align setfacl(1) usage a bit closer to the usage on Linux. Rename -d option to -x, --substitute to --set. Add --no-mask and --mask options. Allow to use the -b and -k option combined to allow reducing an ACL to only reflect standard POSIX permissions.

- Fix (numeric and monetary) decimal point and thousands separator in fa_IR and ps_AF locales to be aligned with Linux.

- utmpname/utmpxname are now defined as int functions as on Linux.

1.7.2 What's new and what changed in 2.3

- strftime(3) supports %s (seconds since Epoch) now.

- posix_madvise(POSIX_MADV_WILLNEED) now utilizes OS functionality available starting with Windows 8/Server 2012. posix_madvise(POSIX_MADV_DONTNEED) now utilizes OS functionality available starting with Windows 8.1/Server 2012R2.

- sysconf() now supports returning CPU cache information:

```
_SC_LEVEL1_ICACHE_SIZE, _SC_LEVEL1_ICACHE_ASSOC, _SC_LEVEL1_ICACHE_LINESIZE,
_SC_LEVEL1_DCACHE_SIZE, _SC_LEVEL1_DCACHE_ASSOC, _SC_LEVEL1_DCACHE_LINESIZE,
_SC_LEVEL2_CACHE_SIZE, _SC_LEVEL2_CACHE_ASSOC, _SC_LEVEL2_CACHE_LINESIZE,
_SC_LEVEL3_CACHE_SIZE, _SC_LEVEL3_CACHE_ASSOC, _SC_LEVEL3_CACHE_LINESIZE,
_SC_LEVEL4_CACHE_SIZE, _SC_LEVEL4_CACHE_ASSOC, _SC_LEVEL4_CACHE_LINESIZE
```

- New API: aligned_alloc, at_quick_exit, quick_exit.

- Add support for Parallels Desktop FS (prlfs).

1.7.3 What's new and what changed in 2.2

- New APIs: getcontext, setcontext, makecontext, swapcontext.

- New functions: sigsetjmp, siglongjmp.

  These were only available as macros up to now, but POSIX requires that siglongjmp has to be available as function.

1.7.4 What's new and what changed in 2.1

- Handle pthread stacksizes as in GLibc: Default to RLIMIT_STACK resource. Allow to set RLIMIT_STACK via setrlimit. Default RLIMIT_STACK to value from executable header as described on the MSDN website Thread Stack Size Default stacksize to 2 Megs in case RLIMIT_STACK is set to RLIM_INFINITY.

- First cut of an implementation to allow signal handlers running on an alternate signal stack.

- New API sigaltstack, plus definitions for SA_ONSTACK, SS_ONSTACK, SS_DISABLE, MINSIGSTKSZ, SIGSTKSZ.

- New API: sethostname.

1.7.5 What's new and what changed in 2.0

- basename(3) now comes in two flavors, POSIX and GNU. The POSIX version is the default. You get the GNU version after

```
#define _GNU_SOURCE
#include <string.h>
```

1.7.6 What's new and what changed in 1.7.35

- Performance improvements of the new account DB handling.

- Since 1.7.34, chmod does not always affect the POSIX permission mask as returned by stat(2) or printed by ls(1), due to the improved POSIX ACL handling. However, that's still far from perfect, so, as a temporary workaround, chmod now checks if secondary groups and users in the ACL have more permissions than the primary group. If so, the permissions of the secondary users and groups will be reduced according to the mask given by the new primary group permissions. I.e, chmod 600 will remove all permissions from the primary group as well as all secondary user and group entries in the ACL.

- Change handling of group permissions if owner SID == group SID. Now the group permissions don't mirror the user permissions anymore, thus leading to less hassle with security-conscious applications.

- Allow group SID to be the same as owner SID for "Microsoft Accounts". Those have the group in their user token set to the owner SID by default. Drop the workaround to change their primary group to "Users". It's not required anymore due to the aforementioned changes.

- Change getfacl long options from --all to --access and from --dir to --default, along the lines of the Linux getfacl tool.

- Don't raise a SIGSYS signal in the XSI IPC functions if cygserver is not running. Just return -1 with errno set to ENOSYS.

- New APIs: cabsl, cimagl, creall, finitel, hypotl, sqrtl.

- New API: issetugid.

1.7.7 What's new and what changed in 1.7.34

- Cygwin can now generate passwd/group entries directly from Windows user databases (local SAM or Active Directory), thus allowing to run Cygwin without having to create /etc/passwd and /etc/group files. Introduce /etc/nsswitch.conf file to configure passwd/group handling.

  For bordercase which require to use /etc/passwd and /etc/group files, change mkpasswd/mkgroup to generate passwd/group entries compatible with the entries read from SAM/AD.

  For a description of this exciting new feature see Section 3.6.

- Add -b/--remove-all option to setfacl to reduce the ACL to only the entries representing POSIX permission bits.

- Add -k/--remove-default option to setfacl to remove all default ACL entries from an ACL.

- Add restore action to regtool.

- Make gethostbyname2 handle numeric host addresses as well as the reserved domain names "localhost" and "invalid" per RFC 6761.

- Revamp Solaris ACL implementation to more closely work like POSIX ACLs are supposed to work. Finally implement a CLASS_OBJ emulation. Update getfacl(1)/setfacl(1) accordingly.

- The xdr functions are no longer exported for newly built executables. Use libtirpc-devel instead.

- 32 bit only: Change default values for socket buffer size to raise performance on 10Gb networks.

- When spawning a process under another user account, merge the user's default Windows environment into the new process' environment.

- New APIs: qsort_r, __bsd_qsort_r.

- New API: wcstold.

- New APIs: __fbufsize, __flbf, __fpending, __freadable, __freading, __fsetlocking, __fwritable, __fwriting.

- New APIs: clearerr_unlocked, feof_unlocked, ferror_unlocked, fflush_unlocked, fgetc_unlocked, fgets_unlocked, fgetwc_unlocked, fgetws_unlocked, fileno_unlocked, fputc_unlocked, fputs_unlocked, fputwc_unlocked, fputws_unlocked, fread_unlocked, fwrite_unlocked, getwc_unlocked, getwchar_unlocked, putwc_unlocked, putwchar_unlocked.

- New API: sockatmark.

1.7.8   What's new and what changed in 1.7.33

- /proc/cygdrive is a new symlink pointing to the current cygdrive prefix. This can be utilized in scripts to access paths via cygdrive prefix, even if the cygdrive prefix has been changed by the user.

- /proc/partitions now prints the windows mount points the device is mounted on. This allows to recognize the underlying Windows devices of the Cygwin raw device names.

- New API: quotactl, designed after the Linux/BSD function, but severely restricted: Windows only supports user block quotas on NTFS, no group quotas, no inode quotas, no time constraints.

- New APIs: ffsl, ffsll (glibc extensions).

- New API: stime (SVr4).

- Provide Cygwin documentation (PDFs and HTML) for offline usage in `/usr/share/doc/cygwin-${version}`.

- New internal exception handling based on SEH on 64 bit Cygwin.

- When exec'ing applications, check if $PATH exists and is non-empty. If not, add PATH variable with Cygwin installation directory as content to Windows environment to allow loading of Cygwin system DLLs.

- Disable CYGWIN "dosfilewarning" option by default.

- Improve various header files for C++- and standards-compliance.

- Doug Lea malloc implementation update from 2.8.3 to the latest 2.8.6.

- atexit(3) is now exported as statically linked function from libcygwin.a. This allows reliable access to the DSO handle of the caller for newly built executables. The former atexit entry point into the DLL remains for backward compatibility only.

1.7.9   What's new and what changed in 1.7.32

- Export __cxa_atexit and __cxa_finalize to allow C++ standards-compliant destructor handling in libstdc++ and g++ compiled code. Please note that, in order to benefit from this new feature, C++ code must be recompiled with the upcoming gcc 4.8.3-3 release which will enable the -fuse-cxa-atexit flag by default, and that C++ applications using this feature will not run on older Cygwin releases.

- Support more recent CPU flags in /proc/cpuinfo.

1.7.10   What's new and what changed in 1.7.31

- Improve performance of send(2), sendto(2), sendmsg(2) when using small input buffers.

- The default pthread_mutex type is now PTHREAD_MUTEX_NORMAL, rather than PTHREAD_MUTEX_ERRORCHECK, just as on Linux.

- Align pthread_attr stack functions more closely to Linux.

- Mark pthread_attr_getstackaddr and pthread_attr_setstackaddr as deprecated, as on Linux.

1.7.11   What's new and what changed in 1.7.29

- Allow quoting of arguments to the CYGWIN environment variable, i.e., set CYGWIN=error_start="c:\bin\someprogram -T"

- Console screen clearing works more like xterm or mintty.

1.7.12   What's new and what changed in 1.7.28

- popen now supports the Glibc 'e' flag to set the FD_CLOEXEC flag on the pipe in a thread-safe way.

- New netinet/ip6.h header.

- Switch to BSD FILE stream fopen/exit semantics, as in all BSD variants and Linux/GLibc: Don't fflush/lseek a FILE stream on fclose and exit, if it only has been read from.

1.7.13   What's new and what changed in 1.7.27

- Don't create native symlinks with target paths having long path prefixes "\\?\" if the target path is shorter than MAX_PATH characters. This works around a Windows 8.1 bug: The ShellExecuteW fails if the lpFile parameter points to a native NTFS symlink with a target path prefixed with "\\?\".

1.7.14   What's new and what changed in 1.7.26

- getaddrinfo now supports glibc-specific International Domain Name (IDN) extension flags: AI_IDN, AI_CANONIDN, AI_IDN_ALLOW_U AI_IDN_USE_STD3_ASCII_RULES.

- getnameinfo now supports glibc-specific International Domain Name (IDN) extension flags: NI_IDN, NI_IDN_ALLOW_UNASSIGNED, NI_IDN_USE_STD3_ASCII_RULES.

- Slightly improve randomness of /dev/random emulation.

- Allow to use advisory locking on any device. POSIX fcntl and lockf locking works with any device, BSD flock locking only with devices backed by an OS handle. Right now this excludes console windows on pre Windows 8, as well as almost all virtual files under /proc from BSD flock locking.

- The header /usr/include/exceptions.h, containing implementation details for 32 bit Windows' exception handling only, has been removed.

- Preliminary, experimental support of the posix_spawn family of functions. New associated header /usr/include/spawn.h.

1.7.15   What's new and what changed in 1.7.25

- Change magic number associated with process information block so that 32-bit Cygwin processes don't try to interpret 64-bit information and vice-versa.

- Redefine content of mtget tape info struct to allow fetching the number of partitions on a tape.

1.7.16 What's new and what changed in 1.7.24

- Allow application override of posix_memalign.

1.7.17 What's new and what changed in 1.7.23

- Added CYGWIN environment variable keyword "wincmdln" which causes Cygwin to send the full windows command line to any subprocesses.

1.7.18 What's new and what changed in 1.7.22

- Support for /dev/mem, /dev/kmem and /dev/port removed, since OS support was limited to 32 bit Windows XP only.

- Added cygwin GetCommandLine wrappers which will allow Cygwin programs to (appear to) use the Windows command line functions.

- regcomp(3) now allows character values >= 0x80 if the current codeset is ASCII (default codeset in the "C"/"POSIX" locale). This allows patterns containing arbitrary byte values as GLibc's regcomp.

1.7.19 What's new and what changed in 1.7.21

- New API: rawmemchr.

1.7.20 What's new and what changed in 1.7.19

- Drop support for Windows 2000 and Windows XP pre-SP3.

- Add support for building a 64 bit version of Cygwin on x86_64 natively.

- Add support for creating native NTFS symlinks starting with Windows Vista by setting the CYGWIN=winsymlinks:native or CYGWIN=winsymlinks:nativestrict option.

- Add support for AFS filesystem.

- Preliminary support for mandatory locking via fcntl/flock/lockf, using Windows locking semantics. New F_LCK_MANDATORY fcntl command.

- New APIs: __b64_ntop, __b64_pton, arc4random, arc4random_addrandom, arc4random_buf, arc4random_stir, arc4random_uniform.

1.7.21 What's new and what changed in 1.7.18

- Added Windows console cursor appearance support.

  - Show/Hide Cursor mode (DECTCEM): "ESC[?25h" / "ESC[?25l"
  - Set cursor style (DECSCUSR): "ESC[n q" (note the space before the q); where n is 0, 1, 2 for block cursor, 3, 4 for underline cursor (all disregarding blinking mode), or > 4 to set the cursor height to a percentage of the cell height.

- For performance reasons, Cygwin does not try to create sparse files automatically anymore, unless you use the new "sparse" mount option.

- New API: cfsetspeed.

1.7.22 What's new and what changed in 1.7.17

- Support the "e" flag to fopen(3). This is a Glibc extension which allows to fopen the file with the O_CLOEXEC flag set.

- Support the "x" flag to fopen(3). This is a Glibc/C11 extension which allows to open the file with the O_EXCL flag set.

1.7.23   What's new and what changed in 1.7.16

- New API: getmntent_r, memrchr.

- Recognize ReFS filesystem.

1.7.24   What's new and what changed in 1.7.15

- CYGWIN=pipe_byte option now forces the opening of pipes in byte mode rather than message mode.

1.7.25   What's new and what changed in 1.7.14

- Add mouse reporting modes 1005, 1006 and 1015 to console window.

1.7.26   What's new and what changed in 1.7.13

- mkpasswd and mkgroup now try to print an entry for the TrustedInstaller account existing since Windows Vista/Server 2008.

- Terminal typeahead when switching from canonical to non-canonical mode is now properly flushed.

1.7.27   What's new and what changed in 1.7.12

- Cygwin now automatically populates the /dev directory with all existing POSIX devices.

- Add virtual /proc/PID/mountinfo file.

- flock now additionally supports the following scenario, which requires to propagate locks to the parent process:

```
(
  flock -n 9 || exit 1
  # ... commands executed under lock ...
} 9>/var/lock/mylockfile
```

  Only propagation to the direct parent process is supported so far, not to grand parents or sibling processes.

- Add a "detect_bloda" setting for the CYGWIN environment variable to help finding potential BLODAs.

1.7.28   What's new and what changed in 1.7.11

- New **pldd** command for listing DLLs loaded by a process.

- New API: scandirat.

- Change the way remote shares mapped to drive letters are recognized when creating the cygdrive directory. If Windows claims the drive is unavailable, don't show it in the cygdrive directory listing.

- Raise default stacksize of pthreads from 512K to 1 Meg. It can still be changed using the pthread_attr_setstacksize call.

1.7.29   What's new and what changed in 1.7.10

- Drop support for Windows NT4.

- The CYGWIN environment variable options "envcache", "strip_title", "title", "tty", and "upcaseenv" have been removed.

- If the executable (and the system) is large address aware, the application heap will be placed in the large memory area. The **peflags** tool from the `rebase` package can be used to set the large address awareness flag in the executable file header.

- The registry setting "heap_chunk_in_mb" has been removed, in favor of a new per-executable setting in the executable file header which can be set using the **peflags** tool. See Section 2.3 for more information.

- The CYGWIN=tty mode using pipes to communicate with the console in a pseudo tty-like mode has been removed. Either just use the normal Windows console as is, or use a terminal application like **mintty**.

- New **getconf** command for querying confstr(3), pathconf(3), sysconf(3), and limits.h configuration.

- New **tzset** utility to generate a POSIX-compatible TZ environment variable from the Windows timezone settings.

- The passwd command now allows an administrator to use the -R command for other user accounts: passwd -R username.

- Pthread spinlocks. New APIs: pthread_spin_destroy, pthread_spin_init, pthread_spin_lock, pthread_spin_trylock, pthread_spin_unlock.

- Pthread stack address management. New APIs: pthread_attr_getstack, pthread_attr_getstackaddr, pthread_attr_getguardsize, pthread_attr_setstack, pthread_attr_setstackaddr, pthread_attr_setguardsize, pthread_getattr_np.

- POSIX Clock Selection option. New APIs: clock_nanosleep, pthread_condattr_getclock, pthread_condattr_setclock.

- clock_gettime(3) and clock_getres(3) accept per-process and per-thread CPU-time clocks, including CLOCK_PROCESS_CPUTIME_ID and CLOCK_THREAD_CPUTIME_ID. New APIs: clock_getcpuclockid, pthread_getcpuclockid.

- GNU/glibc error.h error reporting functions. New APIs: error, error_at_line. New exports: error_message_count, error_one_per_line, error_print_progname. Also, perror and strerror_r no longer clobber strerror storage.

- C99 <tgmath.h> type-generic macros.

- /proc/loadavg now shows the number of currently running processes and the total number of processes.

- Added /proc/devices and /proc/misc, which lists supported device types and their device numbers.

- Added /proc/swaps, which shows the location and size of Windows paging file(s).

- Added /proc/sysvipc/msg, /proc/sysvipc/sem, and /proc/sysvipc/shm which provide information about System V IPC message queues, semaphores, and shared memory.

- /proc/version now shows the username of whomever compiled the Cygwin DLL as well as the version of GCC used when compiling.

- dlopen now supports the Glibc-specific RTLD_NODELETE and RTLD_NOOPEN flags.

- The printf(3) and wprintf(3) families of functions now handle the %m conversion flag.

- Other new API: clock_settime, __fpurge, getgrouplist, get_current_dir_name, getpt, ppoll, psiginfo, psignal, ptsname_r, sys_siglist, pthread_setschedprio, pthread_sigqueue, sysinfo.

1.7.30   What's new and what changed in 1.7.9

- New API: strchrnul.

1.7.31   What's new and what changed in 1.7.8

- Drop support for Windows NT4 prior to Service Pack 4.

- Reinstantiate Cygwin's ability to delete an empty directory which is the current working directory of the same or another process. Same for any other empty directory which has been opened by the same or another process.

- Cygwin now ships the C standard library fenv.h header file, and implements the related APIs (including GNU/glibc extensions): feclearexcept, fedisableexcept, feenableexcept, fegetenv, fegetexcept, fegetexceptflag, fegetprec, fegetround, feholdexcept, feraiseexcept, fesetenv, fesetexceptflag, fesetprec, fesetround, fetestexcept, feupdateenv, and predefines both default and no-mask FP environments. See the GNU C Library manual for full details of this functionality.

- Support for the C99 complex functions, except for the "long double" implementations. New APIs: cacos, cacosf, cacosh, cacoshf, carg, cargf, casin, casinf, casinh, casinhf, catan, catanf, catanh, catanhf, ccos, ccosf, ccosh, ccoshf, cexp, cexpf, cimag, cimagf, clog, clogf, conj, conjf, cpow, cpowf, cproj, cprojf, creal, crealf, csin, csinf, csinh, csinhf, csqrt, csqrtf, ctan, ctanf, ctanh, ctanhf.

- Fix the width of "CJK Ambiguous Width" characters to 1 for singlebyte charsets and 2 for East Asian multibyte charsets. (For UTF-8, it remains dependent on the specified language, and the "@cjknarrow" locale modifier can still be used to force width 1.)

- The strerror_r interface now has two flavors; if _GNU_SOURCE is defined, it retains the previous behavior of returning char * (but the result is now guaranteed to be NUL-terminated); otherwise it now obeys POSIX semantics of returning int.

- /proc/sys now allows unfiltered access to the native NT namespace. Access restrictions still apply. Direct device access via /proc/sys is not yet supported. File system access via block devices works. For instance (note the trailing slash!)

```
bash$ cd /proc/sys/Device/HarddiskVolumeShadowCopy1/
```

- Other new APIs: llround, llroundf, madvise, pthread_yield. Export program_invocation_name, program_invocation_short_name. Support TIOCGPGRP, TIOCSPGRP ioctls.

1.7.32   What's new and what changed in 1.7.7

- Partially revert the 1.7.6 change to set the Win32 current working directory (CWD) always to an invalid directory, since it breaks backward compatibility too much. The Cygwin CWD and the Win32 CWD are now kept in sync again, unless the Cygwin CWD is not usable as Win32 CWD. See the reworked Section 3.1.8 for details.

- Make sure to follow the Microsoft security advisory concerning DLL hijacking. See the Microsoft Security Advisory (2269637) "Insecure Library Loading Could Allow Remote Code Execution" for details.

- Allow to link against -lbinmode instead of /lib/binmode.o. Same for -ltextmode, -ltextreadmode and -lautomode. See Section 3.2.4 for details.

1.7.33   What's new and what changed in 1.7.6

- Add new mount options "dos" and "ihash" to allow overriding Cygwin default behaviour on broken filesystems not recognized by Cygwin.

- Add new mount option "bind" to allow remounting parts of the POSIX file hirarchy somewhere else.

- Ttys and ptys are handled as securable objects using file-like permissions and owner/group information. **chmod** and **chown** now work on ttys/ptys. A new mechanism is used to propagate pty handles safely to other processes, which does not require to use Cygserver.

- Pass on coresize settings made with setrlimit(2). This allows shells to disable creating stackdump files in child processes via

```
ulimit -c 0
```

in bash or

```
limit coredumpsize 0
```

in tcsh.

- Locale categories contain all localization strings additionally as wide-char strings. locale(1) prints these values just as on Linux. nl_langinfo(3) allows to fetch them.

- New interfaces mkostemp(3) and mkostemps(3) are added.

- New virtual file /proc/filesystems.

- clock_gettime(3) and clock_getres(3) accept CLOCK_MONOTONIC.

- DEPRECATED with 1.7.7: Cygwin handles the current working directory entirely on its own. The Win32 current working directory is set to an invalid path to be out of the way. [...]

1.7.34   What's new and what changed in 1.7.5

- Support for DEC Backarrow Key Mode escape sequences (ESC [? 67 h, ESC [? 67 l) in Windows console.

1.7.35   What's new and what changed in 1.7.3

- Support for GB2312/EUC-CN. These charsets are implemented as aliases to GBK. GB2312 is now the default charset name for the locales zh_CN and zh_SG, just as on Linux.

- Modification and access timestamps of devices reflect the current time.

1.7.36   What's new and what changed in 1.7.2

- Localization support has been much improved.

  - Cygwin now handles locales using the underlying Windows locale support. The locale must exist in Windows to be recognized. Locale aliases from the file /usr/share/locale/locale.alias are also allowed, as long as their replacement is supported by the underlying Windows.

  - New tool "locale" to fetch locale information and default locales based on the Windows default settings as well as lists of all supported locales and character sets.

  - Default charset for locales without explicit charset is now chosen from a list of Linux-compatible charsets.
    For instance: en_US -> ISO-8859-1, ja_JP -> EUC-JP, zh_TW -> Big5.

  - Added support for the charsets GEORGIAN-PS, PT154, and TIS-620.

  - Support for the various locale modifiers to switch charsets as on Linux.

  - Default charset in the "C" or "POSIX" locale has been changed back from UTF-8 to ASCII, to avoid problems with applications expecting a singlebyte charset in the "C"/"POSIX" locale. Still use UTF-8 internally for filename conversion in this case.

  - LC_COLLATE, LC_MONETARY, LC_NUMERIC, and LC_TIME localization is enabled via Windows locale support. LC_MESSAGES is enabled via a big table with localized strings.

  - fnmatch(3), regcomp(3), regexec(3) calls are now multibyte-aware.

  - printf(3), wprintf(3) families of functions now handle the grouping flag, the apostrophe ' , per POSIX-1.2008. The integer portion of the result of a decimal conversion (%i, %d, %u, %f, %F, %g, %G) will be formatted with thousands' grouping characters.

  - strftime(3), wcsftime(3), and strptime(3) now handle the E and O format modifiers to print/scan alternative date and time representations or to use alternative digits in locales which support this. Additionally these functions now also support the padding modifiers '0' and '+', as well as a field width per POSIX-1.2008.

  - New strfmon(3) call.

- Support open(2) flags O_CLOEXEC and O_TTY_INIT flags. Support fcntl flag F_DUPFD_CLOEXEC. Support socket flags SOCK_CLOEXEC and SOCK_NONBLOCK. Add new Linux-compatible API calls accept4(2), dup3(2), and pipe2(2). Support the signal SIGPWR.

- Enhanced Windows console support.

  - The console's backspace keycode can be changed using 'stty erase'.

  - Function keys send distinguished escape sequences compatible with rxvt. Keypad keys send distinguished escape sequences, xterm-style.

  - Support of combining Alt and AltGr modifiers in console window (compatible with xterm and mintty), so that e.g. Alt-@ sends ESC @ also on keyboards where @ is mapped to an AltGr combination.

  - Report mouse wheel scroll events in mouse reporting mode 1000 (note: this doesn't seem to work on all systems, assumedly due to driver interworking issues). Add mouse reporting mode 1002 to report mouse drag movement. Add mouse reporting mode 1003 to report any mouse movement. Add focus event reporting (mode 1004), compatible with xterm and mintty.

  - Add escape sequences for not bold (22), not invisible (28), not blinking (25) (compatible with xterm and mintty).

  - Support VT100 line drawing graphics mode in console window (compatible with xterm and mintty).

- Handle native DOS paths always as if mounted with "posix=0,noacl".

- Handle UNC paths starting with slashes identical to /cygdrive paths. In other words, use the /cygdrive mount flags for these paths as well.

- Recognize NWFS filesystem and workaround broken OS call.

- New support for eXtensible Data Record (XDR) encoding and decoding, as defined by RFCs 1014, 1832, and 4506. The XDR protocol and functions are useful for cross-platfrom data exchange, and are commonly used as the core data interchange format for Remote Procedure Call (RPC) and NFS.

1.7.37   What's new and what changed from 1.5 to 1.7

1.7.37.1   OS related changes

- Windows 95, 98 and Me are not supported anymore. The new Cygwin 1.7 DLL will not run on any of these systems.

- Add support for Windows 7 and Windows Server 2008 R2.

1.7.37.2   File Access related changes

- Mount points are no longer stored in the registry. Use /etc/fstab and /etc/fstab.d/$USER instead. Mount points created with mount(1) are only local to the current session and disappear when the last Cygwin process in the session exits.

- Cygwin creates the mount points for /, /usr/bin, and /usr/lib automatically from it's own position on the disk. They don't have to be specified in /etc/fstab.

- If a filename cannot be represented in the current character set, the character will be converted to a sequence Ctrl-X + UTF-8 representation of the character. This allows to access all files, even those not having a valid representation of their filename in the current character set. To always have a valid string, use the UTF-8 charset by setting the environment variable $LANG, $LC_ALL, or $LC_CTYPE to a valid POSIX value, such as "en_US.UTF-8".

- PATH_MAX is now 4096. Internally, path names can be as long as the underlying OS can handle (32K).

- struct dirent now supports d_type, filled out with DT_REG or DT_DIR. All other file types return as DT_UNKNOWN for performance reasons.

- The CYGWIN environment variable options "ntsec" and "smbntsec" have been replaced by the per-mount option "acl"/"noacl".

- The CYGWIN environment variable option "ntea" has been removed without substitute.

- The CYGWIN environment variable option "check_case" has been removed in favor of real case-sensitivity on file systems supporting it.

- Creating filenames with special DOS characters '"', '*', ':', '<', '>', '|' is supported.

- Creating files with special DOS device filename components ("aux", "nul", "prn") is supported.

- File names are case sensitive if the OS and the underlying file system supports it. Works on NTFS and NFS. Does not work on FAT and Samba shares. Requires to change a registry key (see the User's Guide). Can be switched off on a per-mount basis.

- Due to the above changes, managed mounts have been removed.

- Incoming DOS paths are always handled case-insensitive and get no POSIX permission, as if they are mounted with noacl,posix=0 mount flags.

- unlink(2) and rmdir(2) try very hard to remove files/directories even if they are currently accessed or locked. This is done by utilizing the hidden recycle bin directories and marking the files for deletion.

- rename(2) rewritten to be more POSIX conformant.

- access(2) now performs checks using the real user ID, as required by POSIX; the old behavior of querying based on effective user ID is available through the new faccessat(2) and euidaccess(2) APIs.

- Add st_birthtim member to struct stat.

- File locking is now advisory, not mandatory anymore. The fcntl(2) and the new lockf(2) APIs create and maintain locks with POSIX semantics, the flock(2) API creates and maintains locks with BSD semantics. POSIX and BSD locks are independent of each other.

- Implement atomic O_APPEND mode.

- New open(2) flags O_DIRECTORY, O_EXEC and O_SEARCH.

- Make the "plain file with SYSTEM attribute set" style symlink default again when creating symlinks. Only create Windows shortcut style symlinks if CYGWIN=winsymlinks is set in the environment.

- Symlinks now use UTF-16 encoding for the target filename for better internationalization support. Cygwin 1.7 can read all old style symlinks, but the new style is not compatible with older Cygwin releases.

- Handle NTFS native symlinks available since Vista/2008 as symlinks (but don't create Vista/2008 symlinks due to unfortunate OS restrictions).

- Recognize NFS shares and handle them using native mechanisms. Recognize and create real symlinks on NFS shares. Get correct stat(2) information and set real mode bits on open(2), mkdir(2) and chmod(2).

- Recognize MVFS and workaround problems manipulating metadata and handling DOS attributes.

- Recognize Netapp DataOnTap drives and fix inode number handling.

- Recognize Samba version beginning with Samba 3.0.28a using the new extended version information negotiated with the Samba developers.

- Stop faking hardlinks by copying the file on filesystems which don't support hardlinks natively (FAT, FAT32, etc.). Just return an error instead, just like Linux.

- List servers of all accessible domains and workgroups in // instead of just the servers in the own domain/workgroup.

- Support Linux-like extended attributes ([fl]getxattr, [fl]listxattr, [fl]setxattr, [fl]removexattr).

- New file conversion API for conversion from Win32 to POSIX path and vice versa (cygwin_conv_path, cygwin_create_path, cygwin_conv_path_list).

- New openat family of functions: openat, faccessat, fchmodat, fchownat, fstatat, futimesat, linkat, mkdirat, mkfifoat, mknodat, readlinkat, renameat, symlinkat, unlinkat.

- Other new APIs: posix_fadvise, posix_fallocate, funopen, fopencookie, open_memstream, open_wmemstream, fmemopen, fdopendir, fpurge, mkstemps, eaccess, euidaccess, canonicalize_file_name, fexecve, execvpe.

1.7.37.3 Network related changes

- New implementation for blocking sockets and select on sockets which is supposed to allow POSIX-compatible sharing of sockets between threads and processes.

- send/sendto/sendmsg now send data in 64K chunks to circumvent an internal buffer problem in WinSock (KB 201213).

- New send/recv option MSG_DONTWAIT.

- IPv6 support. New APIs getaddrinfo, getnameinfo, freeaddrinfo, gai_strerror, in6addr_any, in6addr_loopback. On IPv6-less systems, replacement functions are available for IPv4. On systems with IPv6 enabled, the underlying WinSock functions are used. While I tried hard to get the functionality as POSIXy as possible, keep in mind that a *fully* conformant implementation of getaddrinfo and other stuff is only available starting with Windows Vista/2008.

- Resolver functions (res_init, res_query, res_search, res_querydomain, res_mkquery, res_send, dn_comp, dn_expand) are now part of Cygwin. Applications don't have to link against minires anymore. Actually, this *is* the former libminires.a.

- rcmd is now implemented inside of Cygwin, instead of calling the WinSock function. This allows rsh(1) usage on Vista/2008 and later, which dropped this function from WinSock.

- Define multicast structures in netinet/in.h. Note that fully conformant multicast support is only available beginning with Vista/2008.

- Improve get_ifconf. Redefine struct ifreq and subsequent datastructures to be able to keep more information. Support SIOCGIFINDEX, SIOCGIFDSTADDR and the Cygwin specific SIOCGIFFRNDLYNAM. Support real interface flags on systems supporting them.

- Other new APIs: bindresvport, bindresvport_sa, gethostbyname2, iruserok_sa, rcmd_af, rresvport_af. getifaddrs, freeifaddrs, if_nametoindex, if_indextoname, if_nameindex, if_freenameindex.

- Add /proc/net/if_inet6.

1.7.37.4 Device related changes

- Reworked pipe implementation which uses overlapped IO to create more reliable interruptible pipes and fifos.

- The CYGWIN environment variable option "binmode" has been removed.

- Improved fifo handling by using native Windows named pipes.

- Detect when a stdin/stdout which looks like a pipe is really a tty. Among other things, this allows a debugged application to recognize that it is using the same tty as the debugger.

- Support UTF-8 in console window.

- In the console window the backspace key now emits DEL (0x7f) instead of BS (0x08), Alt-Backspace emits ESC-DEL (0x1b,0x7f) instead of DEL (0x7f), same as the Linux console and xterm. Control-Space now emits an ASCII NUL (0x0) character.

- Support up to 64 serial interfaces using /dev/ttyS0 - /dev/ttyS63.

- Support up to 128 raw disk drives /dev/sda - /dev/sddx.

- New API: cfmakeraw, get_avphys_pages, get_nprocs, get_nprocs_conf, get_phys_pages, posix_openpt.

1.7.37.5 Other POSIX related changes

- A lot of character sets are supported now via a call to setlocale(). The setting of the environment variables $LANG, $LC_ALL or $LC_CTYPE will be used. For instance, setting $LANG to "de_DE.ISO-8859-15" before starting a Cygwin session will use the ISO-8859-15 character set in the entire session. The default locale in the absence of one of the aforementioned environment variables is "C.UTF-8".

  The full list of supported character sets: "ASCII", "ISO-8859-x" with x in 1-16, except 12, "UTF-8", Windows codepages "CPxxx", with xxx in (437, 720, 737, 775, 850, 852, 855, 857, 858, 862, 866, 874, 1125, 1250, 1251, 1252, 1253, 1254, 1255, 1256, 1257, 1258), "KOI8-R", "KOI8-U", "SJIS", "GBK", "eucJP", "eucKR", and "Big5".

- Allow multiple concurrent read locks per thread for pthread_rwlock_t.

- Implement pthread_kill(thread, 0) as per POSIX.

- New API for POSIX IPC: Named semaphores: sem_open, sem_close, sem_unlink. Message queues: mq_open, mq_getattr, mq_setattr, mq_notify, mq_send, mq_timedsend, mq_receive, mq_timedreceive, mq_close, mq_unlink. Shared memory: shm_open, shm_unlink.

- Only declare expected functions in <strings.h>, don't include <string.h> from here.

- Support for WCONTINUED, WIFCONTINUED() added to waitpid and wait4.

- New APIs: _Exit, confstr, insque, remque, sys_sigabbrev, posix_madvise, posix_memalign, reallocf, exp10, exp10f, pow10, pow10f, lrint, lrintf, rint, rintf, llrint, llrintf, llrintl, lrintl, rintl, mbsnrtowcs, strcasestr, stpcpy, stpncpy, wcpcpy, wcpncpy, wcsnlen, wcsnrtombs, wcsftime, wcstod, wcstof, wcstoimax, wcstok, wcstol, wcstoll, wcstoul, wcstoull, wcstoumax, wcsxfrm, wcscasecmp, wcsncasecmp, fgetwc, fgetws, fputwc, fputws, fwide, getwc, getwchar, putwc, putwchar, ungetwc, asnprintf, dprintf, vasnprintf, vdprintf, wprintf, fwprintf, swprintf, vwprintf, vfwprintf, vswprintf, wscanf, fwscanf, swscanf, vwscanf, vfwscanf, vswscanf.

1.7.37.6 Security related changes

- Getting a domain user's groups is hopefully more bulletproof now.

- Cygwin now comes with a real LSA authentication package. This must be manually installed by a privileged user using the /bin/cyglsa-config script. The advantages and disadvantages are noted in https://cygwin.com/ml/cygwin-developers/2006-11/msg00000.html

- Cygwin now allows storage and use of user passwords in a hidden area of the registry. This is tried first when Cygwin is called by privileged processes to switch the user context. This allows, for instance, ssh public key sessions with full network credentials to access shares on other machines.

- New options have been added to the mkpasswd and mkgroup tools to ease use in multi-machine and multi-domain environments. The existing options have a slightly changed behaviour.

1.7.37.7 Miscellaneous

- New ldd utility, similar to Linux.

- New link libraries libdl.a, libresolv.a, librt.a.

- Fallout from the long path names: If the current working directory is longer than 260 bytes, or if the current working directory is a virtual path (like /proc, /cygdrive, //server), don't call native Win32 programs since they don't understand these paths.

- On the first usage of a DOS path (C:\foo, \\foo\bar), the Cygwin DLL emits a scary warning that DOS paths shouldn't be used. This warning may be disabled via the new CYGWIN=nodosfilewarning setting.

- The CYGWIN environment variable option "server" has been removed. Cygwin automatically uses cygserver if it's available.

- Allow environment of arbitrary size instead of a maximum of 32K.

- Don't force uppercase environment when started from a non-Cygwin process. Except for certain Windows and POSIX variables which are always uppercased, preserve environment case. Switch back to old behaviour with the new CYGWIN=upcaseenv setting.

- Detect and report a missing DLL on process startup.

- Add /proc/registry32 and /proc/registry64 paths to access 32 bit and 64 bit registry on 64 bit systems.

- Add the ability to distinguish registry keys and registry values with the same name in the same registry subtree. The key is called "foo" and the value will be called "foo%val" in this case.

- Align /proc/cpuinfo more closly to Linux content.

- Add /proc/$PID/mounts entries and a symlink /proc/mounts pointing to /proc/self/mounts as on Linux.

- Optimized strstr and memmem implementation.

- Remove backwards compatibility with old signal masks. (Some *very* old programs which use signal masks may no longer work correctly).

- Cygwin now exports wrapper functions for libstdc++ operators new and delete, to support the toolchain in implementing full C++ standards conformance when working with shared libraries.

- Different Cygwin installations in different paths can be run in parallel without knowing of each other. The path of the Cygwin DLL used in a process is a key used when creating IPC objects. So different Cygwin DLLs are running in different namespaces.

- Each Cygwin DLL stores its path and installation key in the registry. This allows troubleshooting of problems which could be a result of having multiple concurrent Cygwin installations.

Chapter 2

Setting Up Cygwin

2.1   Internet Setup

To install the Cygwin net release, go to `https://cygwin.com/` and run either setup-x86.exe to install the 32 bit version of Cygwin, or setup-x86_64.exe to install the 64 bit version of Cygwin. This will download a GUI installer which can be run to download a complete cygwin installation via the internet. Follow the instructions on each screen to install Cygwin.

Note For easier reading the installer is called **setup.exe** throughout the following sections. This refers likewise to both installer applications, setup-x86.exe for 32 bit, as well as setup-x86_64.exe for 64 bit. Apart from the target architecture they are the same thing.

The **setup.exe** installer is designed to be easy for new users to understand while remaining flexible for the experienced. The volunteer development team is constantly working on **setup.exe**; before requesting a new feature, check the wishlist in the GIT README . It may already be present in the GIT version!

On Windows Vista and later, **setup.exe** will check by default if it runs with administrative privileges and, if not, will try to elevate the process. If you want to avoid this behaviour and install under an unprivileged account just for your own usage, run **setup.exe** with the `--no-admin` option.

Since the default value for each option is the logical choice for most installations, you can get a working minimal Cygwin environment installed by simply clicking the Next button at each page. The only exception to this is choosing a Cygwin mirror, which you can choose by experimenting with those listed at `https://cygwin.com/mirrors.html`. For more details about each of page of the **setup.exe** installation, read on below. Please note that this guide assumes that you have a basic understanding of Unix (or a Unix-like OS). If you are new to Unix, you will also want to make use of other resources.

2.1.1   Download Source

Cygwin uses packages to manage installing various software. When the default `Install from Internet` option is chosen, **setup.exe** creates a local directory to store the packages before actually installing the contents. `Download from Internet` performs only the first part (storing the packages locally), while `Install from Local Directory` performs only the second (installing the contents of the packages).

The `Download from Internet` option is mainly for creating a base Cygwin package tree on one computer for installation on several machines with `Install from Local Directory`; copy the entire local package tree to another machine with the directory tree intact. For example, you might create a `C:\cache\` directory and place **setup.exe** in it. Run **setup.exe** to `Install from Internet` or `Download from Internet`, then copy the whole `C:\cache\` to each machine and instead choose `Install from Local Directory`.

Though this provides some basic mirroring functionality, if you are managing a large Cygwin installation, to keep up to date we recommend using a mirroring tool such as **wget**. A helpful user on the Cygwin mailing list created a simple demonstration script to accomplish this; search the list for **mkcygwget** for ideas.

2.1.2 Selecting an Install Directory

The `Root Directory` for Cygwin (default `C:\cygwin`) will become / within your Cygwin installation. You must have write access to the parent directory, and any ACLs on the parent directory will determine access to installed files.

The `Install For` options of `All Users` or `Just Me` should always be left on the default `All Users`, unless you do not have write access to `HKEY_LOCAL_MACHINE` in the registry or the All Users Start Menu. This is true even if you are the only user planning to use Cygwin on the machine. Selecting `Just Me` will cause problems for programs such as **crond** and **sshd**. If you do not have the necessary permissions, but still want to use these programs, consult the Cygwin mailing list archives about others' experiences.

2.1.3 Local Package Directory

The `Local Package Directory` is the cache where **setup.exe** stores the packages before they are installed. The cache must not be the same folder as the Cygwin root. Within the cache, a separate directory is created for each Cygwin mirror, which allows **setup.exe** to use multiple mirrors and custom packages. After installing Cygwin, the cache is no longer necessary, but you may want to retain the packages as backups, for installing Cygwin to another system, or in case you need to reinstall a package.

2.1.4 Connection Method

The `Direct Connection` method of downloading will directly download the packages, while the IE5 method will leverage your IE5 cache for performance. If your organisation uses a proxy server or auto-configuration scripts, the IE5 method also uses these settings. If you have a proxy server, you can manually type it into the `Use Proxy` section. Unfortunately, **setup.exe** does not currently support password authorization for proxy servers.

2.1.5 Choosing Mirrors

Since there is no way of knowing from where you will be downloading Cygwin, you need to choose at least one mirror site. Cygwin mirrors are geographically distributed around the world; check the list at `https://cygwin.com/mirrors.html` to find one near you. You can select multiple mirrors by holding down CTRL and clicking on each one. If you have the URL of an unlisted mirror (for example, if your organization has an internal Cygwin mirror) you can add it.

2.1.6 Choosing Packages

For each selected mirror site, **setup.exe** downloads a small text file called `setup.bz2` that contains a list of packages available from that site along with some basic information about each package which **setup.exe** parses and uses to create the chooser window. For details about the format of this file, see the setup.exe homepage.

The chooser is the most complex part of **setup.exe**. Packages are grouped into categories, and one package may belong to multiple categories (assigned by the volunteer package maintainer). Each package can be found under any of those categories in the hierarchical chooser view. By default, **setup.exe** will install only the packages in the `Base` category and their dependencies, resulting in a minimal Cygwin installation. However, this will not include many commonly used tools such as **gcc** (which you will find in the `Devel` category). Since **setup.exe** automatically selects dependencies, be careful not to unselect any required packages. In particular, everything in the `Base` category is required.

You can change **setup.exe**'s view style, which is helpful if you know the name of a package you want to install but not which category it is in. Click on the `View` button and it will rotate between `Category` (the default), `Full` (all packages), and `Pending` (only packages to be installed, removed or upgraded). If you are familiar with Unix, you will probably want to at least glance through the `Full` listing for your favorite tools.

Once you have an existing Cygwin installation, the **setup.exe** chooser is also used to manage your Cygwin installation. Information on installed packages is kept in the `/etc/setup/` directory of your Cygwin installation; if **setup.exe** cannot find this directory it will act as if you have no Cygwin installation. If **setup.exe** finds a newer version of an installed package available, it will automatically mark it to be upgraded. To `Uninstall`, `Reinstall`, or get the `Source` for an existing package, click on `Keep` to toggle it. Also, to avoid the need to reboot after upgrading, make sure to close all Cygwin windows and stop all Cygwin processes before **setup.exe** begins to install the upgraded package.

To avoid unintentionally upgrading, use the `Pending` view to see which packages have been marked for upgrading. If you don't want to upgrade a package, click on the new version number to toggle it until it says `Keep`. All packages can be set to stay at the installed version by pressing the `Keep` button in the top right part of the chooser window.

A previous version of each package is usually available, in case downgrading is required to avoid a serious bug in the current version of the package. Packages also occasionally have testing (or "experimental") versions available. Previous and experimental versions can be chosen by clicking on the package's `New` column until the required version appears.

All available experimental packages can be selected by pressing the `Exp` in the top right part of the chooser window. Be warned, however, that the next time you run **setup.exe** it will try to replace all old or experimental versions with the current version, unless told otherwise.

2.1.7   Download and Installation Progress

First, **setup.exe** will download all selected packages to the local directory chosen earlier. Before installing, **setup.exe** performs a checksum on each package. If the local directory is a slow medium (such as a network drive) this can take a long time. During the download and installation, **setup.exe** shows progress bars for the current task and total remaining disk space.

2.1.8   Shortcuts

You may choose to install "Cygwin Terminal" shortcuts on the Desktop and/or Start Menu. These shortcuts run **mintty**, which will start your default shell as specified in `/etc/passwd`.

2.1.9   Post-Install Scripts

Last of all, **setup.exe** will run any post-install scripts to finish correctly setting up installed packages. Since each script is run separately, several windows may pop up. If you are interested in what is being done, see the Cygwin Package Contributor's Guide at `https://cygwin.com/setup.html` When the last post-install script is completed, **setup.exe** will display a box announcing the completion. A few packages, such as the OpenSSH server, require some manual site-specific configuration. Relevant documentation can be found in the `/usr/doc/Cygwin/` or `/usr/share/doc/Cygwin/` directory.

2.1.10   Troubleshooting

Unfortunately, the complex setup process means that odd problems can occur. If you're having trouble downloading packages, it may be network congestion, so try a different mirror and/or a different protocol (i.e., HTTP instead of FTP). If you notice something is not working after running setup, you can check the **setup.exe** log file at `/var/log/setup.log.full`. Make a backup of this file before running **setup.exe** again, and follow the steps for Reporting Problems with Cygwin.

2.2   Environment Variables

2.2.1   Overview

All Windows environment variables are imported when Cygwin starts. Apart from that, you may wish to specify settings of several important environment variables that affect Cygwin's operation.

The `CYGWIN` variable is used to configure a few global settings for the Cygwin runtime system. Typically you can leave `CYGWIN` unset, but if you want to set one ore more options, you can set it using a syntax like this, depending on the shell in which you're setting it. Here is an example in CMD syntax:

```
C:\> set CYGWIN=error_start:C:\cygwin\bin\gdb.exe glob
```

This is, of course, just an example. For the recognized settings of the CYGWIN environment variable, see Section 3.5.

Locale support is controlled by the LANG and LC_xxx environment variables. Since Cygwin 1.7.2, all of them are honored and have a meaning. For a more detailed description see Section 2.4.

The PATH environment variable is used by Cygwin applications as a list of directories to search for executable files to run. This environment variable is converted from Windows format (e.g. C:\Windows\system32;C:\Windows) to UNIX format (e.g., /cygdrive/c/Windows/system32:/cygdrive/c/Windows) when a Cygwin process first starts. Set it so that it contains at least the x:\cygwin\bin directory where "x:\cygwin is the "root" of your cygwin installation if you wish to use cygwin tools outside of bash. This is usually done by the batch file you're starting your shell with.

The HOME environment variable is used by many programs to determine the location of your home directory. This environment variable, if it exists, is converted from Windows format when a Cygwin process first starts. However, it's usually set in the shell profile scripts in the /etc directory, and it's **not** recommended to set the variable in your Windows environment.

The TERM environment variable specifies your terminal type. It is automatically set to cygwin if you have not set it to something else.

The LD_LIBRARY_PATH environment variable is used by the Cygwin function dlopen () as a list of directories to search for .dll files to load. This environment variable is converted from Windows format to UNIX format when a Cygwin process first starts. Most Cygwin applications do not make use of the dlopen () call and do not need this variable.

In addition to PATH, HOME, and LD_LIBRARY_PATH, there are three other environment variables which, if they exist in the Windows environment, are converted to UNIX format: TMPDIR, TMP, and TEMP. The first is not set by default in the Windows environment but the other two are, and they point to the default Windows temporary directory. If set, these variables will be used by some Cygwin applications, possibly with unexpected results. You may therefore want to unset them by adding the following two lines to your ~/.bashrc file:

```
unset TMP
unset TEMP
```

This is done in the default ~/.bashrc file. Alternatively, you could set TMP and TEMP to point to /tmp or to any other temporary directory of your choice. For example:

```
export TMP=/tmp
export TEMP=/tmp
```

2.2.2 Restricted Win32 environment

There is a restriction when calling Win32 API functions which require a fully set up application environment. Cygwin maintains its own environment in POSIX style. The Win32 environment is usually stripped to a bare minimum and not at all kept in sync with the Cygwin POSIX environment.

If you need the full Win32 environment set up in a Cygwin process, you have to call

```
#include <sys/cygwin.h>

cygwin_internal (CW_SYNC_WINENV);
```

to synchronize the Win32 environment with the Cygwin environment. Note that this only synchronizes the Win32 environment once with the Cygwin environment. Later changes using the setenv or putenv calls are not reflected in the Win32 environment. In these cases, you have to call the aforementioned cygwin_internal call again.

2.3 Changing Cygwin's Maximum Memory

Cygwin's heap is extensible. However, it does start out at a fixed size and attempts to extend it may run into memory which has been previously allocated by Windows. In some cases, this problem can be solved by changing a field in the file header which is utilized by Cygwin since version 1.7.10 to keep the initial size of the application heap. If the field contains 0, which is the default, the application heap defaults to a size of 384 Megabyte. If the field is set to any other value between 4 and 2048, Cygwin tries to reserve as much Megabytes for the application heap. The field used for this is the "LoaderFlags" field in the NT-specific PE header structure ((`IMAGE_NT_HEADER`)->`OptionalHeader.LoaderFlags`).

This value can be changed for any executable by using a more recent version of the **peflags** tool from the `rebase` Cygwin package. Example:

```
$ peflags --cygwin-heap foo.exe
foo.exe: initial Cygwin heap size: 0 (0x0) MB
$ peflags --cygwin-heap=500 foo.exe
foo.exe: initial Cygwin heap size: 500 (0x1f4) MB
```

Heap memory can be allocated up to the size of the biggest available free block in the processes virtual memory (VM). By default, the VM per process is 2 GB for 32 processes. To get more VM for a process, the executable must have the "large address aware" flag set in the file header. You can use the aforementioned **peflags** tool to set this flag. On 64 bit systems this results in a 4 GB VM for a process started from that executable. On 32 bit systems you also have to prepare the system to allow up to 3 GB per process. See the Microsoft article 4-Gigabyte Tuning for more information.

Note

Older Cygwin releases only supported a global registry setting to change the initial heap size for all Cygwin processes. This setting is not used anymore. However, if you're running an older Cygwin release than 1.7.10, you can add the `DWORD` value `heap_chunk_in_mb` and set it to the desired memory limit in decimal MB. You have to stop all Cygwin processes for this setting to have any effect. It is preferred to do this in Cygwin using the **regtool** program included in the Cygwin package. (see regtool(1)) This example sets the memory limit to 1024 MB for all Cygwin processes (use HKCU instead of HKLM if you want to set this only for the current user):

```
$ regtool -i set /HKLM/Software/Cygwin/heap_chunk_in_mb 1024
$ regtool -v list /HKLM/Software/Cygwin
```

2.4 Internationalization

2.4.1 Overview

Internationalization support is controlled by the `LANG` and `LC_xxx` environment variables. You can set all of them but Cygwin itself only honors the variables `LC_ALL`, `LC_CTYPE`, and `LANG`, in this order, according to the POSIX standard. The content of these variables should follow the POSIX standard for a locale specifier. The correct form of a locale specifier is

```
language[[_TERRITORY][.charset][@modifier]]
```

"language" is a lowercase two character string per ISO 639-1, or, if there is no ISO 639-1 code for the language (for instance, "Lower Sorbian"), a three character string per ISO 639-3.

"TERRITORY" is an uppercase two character string per ISO 3166, charset is one of a list of supported character sets. The modifier doesn't matter here (though some are recognized, see below). If you're interested in the exact description, you can find it in the online publication of the POSIX manual pages on the homepage of the Open Group.

Typical locale specifiers are

```
"de_CH"       language = German, territory = Switzerland, default charset
"fr_FR.UTF-8" language = french, territory = France, charset = UTF-8
"ko_KR.eucKR" language = korean, territory = South Korea, charset = eucKR
"syr_SY"      language = Syriac, territory = Syria, default charset
```

If the locale specifier does not follow the above form, Cygwin checks if the locale is one of the locale aliases defined in the file `/usr/share/locale/locale.alias`. If so, and if the replacement localename is supported by the underlying Windows, the locale is accepted, too. So, given the default content of the `/usr/share/locale/locale.alias` file, the below examples would be valid locale specifiers as well.

```
"catalan"        defined as "ca_ES.ISO-8859-1" in locale.alias
"japanese"       defined as "ja_JP.eucJP"      in locale.alias
"turkish"        defined as "tr_TR.ISO-8859-9" in locale.alias
```

The file /usr/share/locale/locale.alias is provided by the gettext package under Cygwin.

At application startup, the application's locale is set to the default "C" or "POSIX" locale. Under Cygwin 1.7.2 and later, this locale defaults to the ASCII character set on the application level. If you want to stick to the "C" locale and only change to another charset, you can define this by setting one of the locale environment variables to "C.charset". For instance

```
"C.ISO-8859-1"
```

Note

The default locale in the absence of the aforementioned locale environment variables is "C.UTF-8".

Windows uses the UTF-16 charset exclusively to store the names of any object used by the Operating System. This is especially important with filenames. Cygwin uses the setting of the locale environment variables LC_ALL, LC_CTYPE, and LANG, to determine how to convert Windows filenames from their UTF-16 representation to the singlebyte or multibyte character set used by Cygwin.

The setting of the locale environment variables at process startup is effective for Cygwin's internal conversions to and from the Windows UTF-16 object names for the entire lifetime of the current process. Changing the environment variables to another value changes the way filenames are converted in subsequently started child processes, but not within the same process.

However, even if one of the locale environment variables is set to some other value than "C", this does *only* affect how Cygwin itself converts filenames. As the POSIX standard requires, it's the application's responsibility to activate that locale for its own purposes, typically by using the call

```
setlocale (LC_ALL, "");
```

early in the application code. Again, so that this doesn't get lost: If the application calls setlocale as above, and there is none of the important locale variables set in the environment, the locale is set to the default locale, which is "C.UTF-8".

But what about applications which are not locale-aware? Per POSIX, they are running in the "C" or "POSIX" locale, which implies the ASCII charset. The Cygwin DLL itself, however, will nevertheless use the locale set in the environment (or the "C.UTF-8" default locale) for converting filenames etc.

When the locale in the environment specifies an ASCII charset, for example "C" or "en_US.ASCII", Cygwin will still use UTF-8 under the hood to translate filenames. This allows for easier interoperability with applications running in the default "C.UTF-8" locale.

Starting with Cygwin 1.7.2, the language and territory are used to fetch locale-dependent information from Windows. If the language and territory are not known to Windows, the setlocale function fails.

The following modifiers are recognized. Any other modifier is simply ignored for now.

- For locales which use the Euro (EUR) as currency, the modifier "@euro" can be added to enforce usage of the ISO-8859-15 character set, which includes a character for the "Euro" currency sign.

- The default script used for all Serbian language locales (sr_BA, sr_ME, sr_RS, and the deprecated sr_CS and sr_SP) is cyrillic. With the "@latin" modifier it gets switched to the latin script with the respective collation behaviour.

- The default charset of the "be_BY" locale (Belarusian/Belarus) is CP1251. With the "@latin" modifier it's UTF-8.

- The default charset of the "tt_RU" locale (Tatar/Russia) is ISO-8859-5. With the "@iqtelif" modifier it's UTF-8.

- The default charset of the "uz_UZ" locale (Uzbek/Uzbekistan) is ISO-8859-1. With the "@cyrillic" modifier it's UTF-8.

- There's a class of characters in the Unicode character set, called the "CJK Ambiguous Width" characters. For these characters, the width returned by the wcwidth/wcswidth functions is usually 1. This can be a problem with East-Asian languages, which historically use character sets where these characters have a width of 2. Therefore, wcwidth/wcswidth return 2 as the width of these characters when an East-Asian charset such as GBK or SJIS is selected, or when UTF-8 is selected and the language is specified as "zh" (Chinese), "ja" (Japanese), or "ko" (Korean). This is not correct in all circumstances, hence the locale modifier "@cjknarrow" can be used to force wcwidth/wcswidth to return 1 for the ambiguous width characters.

2.4.2 How to set the locale

- Assume that you've set one of the aforementioned environment variables to some valid POSIX locale value, other than "C" and "POSIX". Assume further that you're living in Japan. You might want to use the language code "ja" and the territory "JP", thus setting, say, LANG to "ja_JP". You didn't set a character set, so what will Cygwin use now? Starting with Cygwin 1.7.2, the default character set is determined by the default Windows ANSI codepage for this language and territory. Cygwin uses a character set which is the typical Unix-equivalent to the Windows ANSI codepage. For instance:

```
"en_US"    ISO-8859-1
"el_GR"    ISO-8859-7
"pl_PL"    ISO-8859-2
"pl_PL@euro"    ISO-8859-15
"ja_JP"    EUCJP
"ko_KR"    EUCKR
"te_IN"    UTF-8
```

- You don't want to use the default character set? In that case you have to specify the charset explicitly. For instance, assume you're from Japan and don't want to use the japanese default charset EUC-JP, but the Windows default charset SJIS. What you can do, for instance, is to set the LANG variable in the **mintty** Cygwin Terminal in the "Text" section of its "Options" dialog. If you're starting your Cygwin session via a batch file or a shortcut to a batch file, you can also just set LANG there:

```
@echo off

C:
chdir C:\cygwin\bin
set LANG=ja_JP.SJIS
bash --login -i
```

Note

For a list of locales supported by your Windows machine, use the new **locale -a** command, which is part of the Cygwin package. For a description see locale(1)

Note

For a list of supported character sets, see Section 2.4.5

- Last, but not least, most singlebyte or doublebyte charsets have a big disadvantage. Windows filesystems use the Unicode character set in the UTF-16 encoding to store filename information. Not all characters from the Unicode character set are available in a singlebyte or doublebyte charset. While Cygwin has a workaround to access files with unusual characters (see Section 3.4.4), a better workaround is to use always the UTF-8 character set.

  UTF-8 is the only multibyte character set which can represent every Unicode character.

```
set LANG=es_MX.UTF-8
```

For a description of the Unicode standard, see the homepage of the Unicode Consortium.

2.4.3 The Windows Console character set

Sometimes the Windows console is used to run Cygwin applications. While terminal emulations like the Cygwin Terminal **mintty** or **xterm** have a distinct way to set the character set used for in- and output, the Windows console hasn't such a way, since it's not an application in its own right.

This problem is solved in Cygwin as follows. When a Cygwin process is started in a Windows console (either explicitly from cmd.exe, or implicitly by, for instance, running the C:\cygwin\Cygwin.bat batch file), the Console character set is determined by the setting of the aforementioned internationalization environment variables, the same way as described in Section 2.4.2.

What is that good for? Why not switch the console character set with the applications requirements? After all, the application knows if it uses localization or not. However, what if a non-localized application calls a remote application which itself is localized? This can happen with **ssh** or **rlogin**. Both commands don't have and don't need localization and they never call `setlocale`. Setting one of the internationalization environment variable to the same charset as the remote machine before starting **ssh** or **rlogin** fixes that problem.

2.4.4 Potential Problems when using Locales

You can set the above internationalization variables not only when starting the first Cygwin process, but also in your Cygwin shell on the fly, even switch to yet another character set, and yet another. In bash for instance:

```
bash$ export LC_CTYPE="nl_BE.UTF-8"
```

However, here's a problem. At the start of the first Cygwin process in a session, the Windows environment is converted from UTF-16 to UTF-8. The environment is another of the system objects stored in UTF-16 in Windows.

As long as the environment only contains ASCII characters, this is no problem at all. But if it contains native characters, and you're planning to use, say, GBK, the environment will result in invalid characters in the GBK charset. This would be especially a problem in variables like `PATH`. To circumvent the worst problems, Cygwin converts the `PATH` environment variable to the charset set in the environment, if it's different from the UTF-8 charset.

Note

Per POSIX, the name of an environment variable should only consist of valid ASCII characters, and only of uppercase letters, digits, and the underscore for maximum portability.

Symbolic links, too, may pose a problem when switching charsets on the fly. A symbolic link contains the filename of the target file the symlink points to. When a symlink had been created with older versions of Cygwin, the current ANSI or OEM character set had been used to store the target filename, dependent on the old `CYGWIN` environment variable setting `codepage` (see Section 3.5.2. If the target filename contains non-ASCII characters and you use another character set than your default ANSI/OEM charset, the target filename of the symlink is now potentially an invalid character sequence in the new character set. This behaviour is not different from the behaviour in other Operating Systems. So, if you suddenly can't access a symlink anymore which worked all these years before, maybe it's because you switched to another character set. This doesn't occur with symlinks created with Cygwin 1.7 or later.

Another problem you might encounter is that older versions of Windows did not install all charsets by default. If you are running Windows XP or older, you can open the "Regional and Language Options" portion of the Control Panel, select the "Advanced" tab, and select entries from the "Code page conversion tables" list. The following entries are useful to cygwin: 932/SJIS, 936/GBK, 949/EUC-KR, 950/Big5, 20932/EUC-JP.

2.4.5 List of supported character sets

Last but not least, here's the list of currently supported character sets. The left-hand expression is the name of the charset, as you would use it in the internationalization environment variables as outlined above. Note that charset specifiers are case-insensitive. `EUCJP` is equivalent to `eucJP` or `eUcJp`. Writing the charset in the exact case as given in the list below is a good convention, though.

The right-hand side is the number of the equivalent Windows codepage as well as the Windows name of the codepage. They are only noted here for reference. Don't try to use the bare codepage number or the Windows name of the codepage as charset in locale specifiers, unless they happen to be identical with the left-hand side. Especially in case of the "CPxxx" style charsets, always use them with the trailing "CP".

This works:

```
set LC_ALL=en_US.CP437
```

This does *not* work:

```
set LC_ALL=en_US.437
```

You can find a full list of Windows codepages on the Microsoft MSDN page Code Page Identifiers.

```
Charset                   Codepage
-------------------       --------------------------------------------
ASCII                     20127 (US_ASCII)

CP437                       437 (OEM United States)
CP720                       720 (DOS Arabic)
CP737                       737 (OEM Greek)
CP775                       775 (OEM Baltic)
CP850                       850 (OEM Latin 1, Western European)
CP852                       852 (OEM Latin 2, Central European)
CP855                       855 (OEM Cyrillic)
CP857                       857 (OEM Turkish)
CP858                       858 (OEM Latin 1 + Euro Symbol)
CP862                       862 (OEM Hebrew)
CP866                       866 (OEM Russian)
CP874                       874 (ANSI/OEM Thai)
CP932             932 (Shift_JIS, not exactly identical to SJIS)
CP1125                     1125 (OEM Ukraine)
CP1250                     1250 (ANSI Central European)
CP1251                     1251 (ANSI Cyrillic)
CP1252                     1252 (ANSI Latin 1, Western European)
CP1253                     1253 (ANSI Greek)
CP1254                     1254 (ANSI Turkish)
CP1255                     1255 (ANSI Hebrew)
CP1256                     1256 (ANSI Arabic)
CP1257                     1257 (ANSI Baltic)
CP1258                     1258 (ANSI/OEM Vietnamese)

ISO-8859-1                28591 (ISO-8859-1)
ISO-8859-2                28592 (ISO-8859-2)
ISO-8859-3                28593 (ISO-8859-3)
ISO-8859-4                28594 (ISO-8859-4)
ISO-8859-5                28595 (ISO-8859-5)
ISO-8859-6                28596 (ISO-8859-6)
ISO-8859-7                28597 (ISO-8859-7)
ISO-8859-8                28598 (ISO-8859-8)
ISO-8859-9                28599 (ISO-8859-9)
ISO-8859-10                   -  (not available)
ISO-8859-11                   -  (not available)
ISO-8859-13               28603 (ISO-8859-13)
ISO-8859-14                   -  (not available)
ISO-8859-15               28605 (ISO-8859-15)
ISO-8859-16                   -  (not available)

Big5                        950 (ANSI/OEM Traditional Chinese)
EUCCN or euc-CN             936 (ANSI/OEM Simplified Chinese)
EUCJP or euc-JP           20932 (EUC Japanese)
EUCKR or euc-KR            949 (EUC Korean)
GB2312                      936 (ANSI/OEM Simplified Chinese)
GBK                         936 (ANSI/OEM Simplified Chinese)
GEORGIAN-PS                   -  (not available)
KOI8-R                    20866 (KOI8-R Russian Cyrillic)
KOI8-U                    21866 (KOI8-U Ukrainian Cyrillic)
PT154                        -  (not available)
SJIS                         -  (not available, almost, but not exactly CP932)
TIS620 or TIS-620           874 (ANSI/OEM Thai)
```

```
   UTF-8 or utf8          65001 (UTF-8)
```

2.5 Customizing bash

To set up bash so that cut and paste work properly, click on the "Properties" button of the window, then on the "Misc" tab. Make sure that "QuickEdit mode" and "Insert mode" are checked. These settings will be remembered next time you run bash from that shortcut.

Your home directory should contain three initialization files that control the behavior of bash. They are `.profile`, `.bashrc` and `.inputrc`. The Cygwin base installation creates stub files when you start bash for the first time.

`.profile` (other names are also valid, see the bash man page) contains bash commands. It is executed when bash is started as login shell, e.g. from the command **bash --login**. This is a useful place to define and export environment variables and bash functions that will be used by bash and the programs invoked by bash. It is a good place to redefine `PATH` if needed. We recommend adding a ":." to the end of `PATH` to also search the current working directory (contrary to DOS, the local directory is not searched by default). Also to avoid delays you should either **unset** `MAILCHECK` or define `MAILPATH` to point to your existing mail inbox.

`.bashrc` is similar to `.profile` but is executed each time an interactive bash shell is launched. It serves to define elements that are not inherited through the environment, such as aliases. If you do not use login shells, you may want to put the contents of `.profile` as discussed above in this file instead.

```
shopt -s nocaseglob
```

will allow bash to glob filenames in a case-insensitive manner. Note that `.bashrc` is not called automatically for login shells. You can source it from `.profile`.

`.inputrc` controls how programs using the readline library (including **bash**) behave. It is loaded automatically. For full details see the `Function and Variable Index` section of the GNU `readline` manual. Consider the following settings:

```
# Ignore case while completing
set completion-ignore-case on
# Make Bash 8bit clean
set meta-flag on
set convert-meta off
set output-meta on
```

The first command makes filename completion case insensitive, which can be convenient in a Windows environment. The next three commands allow **bash** to display 8-bit characters, useful for languages with accented characters. Note that tools that do not use `readline` for display, such as **less** and **ls**, require additional settings, which could be put in your `.bashrc`:

```
alias less='/bin/less -r'
alias ls='/bin/ls -F --color=tty --show-control-chars'
```

Chapter 3

Using Cygwin

This chapter explains some key differences between the Cygwin environment and traditional UNIX systems. It assumes a working knowledge of standard UNIX commands.

3.1 Mapping path names

3.1.1 Introduction

Cygwin supports both POSIX- and Win32-style paths. Directory delimiters may be either forward slashes or backslashes. Paths using backslashes or starting with a drive letter are always handled as Win32 paths. POSIX paths must only use forward slashes as delimiter, otherwise they are treated as Win32 paths and file access might fail in surprising ways.

Note

The usage of Win32 paths, though possible, is deprecated, since it circumvents important internal path handling mechanisms. See Section 3.1.7 and Section 3.1.8 for more information.

POSIX operating systems (such as Linux) do not have the concept of drive letters. Instead, all absolute paths begin with a slash (instead of a drive letter such as "c:") and all file systems appear as subdirectories (for example, you might buy a new disk and make it be the /disk2 directory).

Because many programs written to run on UNIX systems assume the existence of a single unified POSIX file system structure, Cygwin maintains a special internal POSIX view of the Win32 file system that allows these programs to successfully run under Windows. Cygwin uses this mapping to translate from POSIX to Win32 paths as necessary.

3.1.2 The Cygwin Mount Table

The /etc/fstab file is used to map Win32 drives and network shares into Cygwin's internal POSIX directory tree. This is a similar concept to the typical UNIX fstab file. The mount points stored in /etc/fstab are globally set for all users. Sometimes there's a requirement to have user specific mount points. The Cygwin DLL supports user specific fstab files. These are stored in the directory /etc/fstab.d and the name of the file is the Cygwin username of the user, as it's created from the Windows account database or stored in the /etc/passwd file (see Section 3.6.2). The structure of the user specific file is identical to the system-wide fstab file.

The file fstab contains descriptive information about the various file systems. fstab is only read by programs, and not written; it is the duty of the system administrator to properly create and maintain this file. Each filesystem is described on a separate line; fields on each line are separated by tabs or spaces. Lines starting with '#' are comments.

The first field describes the block special device or remote filesystem to be mounted. On Cygwin, this is the native Windows path which the mount point links in. As path separator you MUST use a slash. Usage of a backslash might lead to unexpected results. UNC paths (using slashes, not backslashes) are allowed. If the path contains spaces these can be escaped as ' \040'.

The second field describes the mount point for the filesystem. If the name of the mount point contains spaces these can be escaped as '\040'.

The third field describes the type of the filesystem. Cygwin supports any string here, since the file system type is usually not evaluated. So it doesn't matter if you write FAT into this field even if the filesystem is NTFS. Cygwin figures out the filesystem type and its capabilities by itself.

The only two exceptions are the file system types cygdrive and usertemp. The cygdrive type is used to set the cygdrive prefix. For a description of the cygdrive prefix see Section 3.1.4, for a description of the usertemp file system type see Section 3.1.5

The fourth field describes the mount options associated with the filesystem. It is formatted as a comma separated list of options. It contains at least the type of mount (binary or text) plus any additional options appropriate to the filesystem type. The list of the options, including their meaning, follows.

```
acl         - Cygwin uses the filesystem's access control lists (ACLs) to
               implement real POSIX permissions (default).  This flag only
            affects filesystems supporting ACLs (NTFS, for instance) and
            is ignored otherwise.
auto        - Ignored.
binary      - Files default to binary mode (default).
bind        - Allows to remount part of the file hierarchy somewhere else.
               In contrast to other entries, the first field in the fstab
            line specifies an absolute POSIX path.  This path is remounted
            to the POSIX path specified as the second path.  The conversion
            to a Win32 path is done on the fly.  Only the root path and
            paths preceding the bind entry in the fstab file are used to
            convert the POSIX path in the first field to an absolute Win32
            path.  Note that symlinks are ignored while performing this path
            conversion.
cygexec     - Treat all files below mount point as cygwin executables.
dos         - Always convert leading spaces and trailing dots and spaces to
            characters in the UNICODE private use area.  This allows to use
            broken filesystems which only allow DOS filenames, even if they
            are not recognized as such by Cygwin.
exec        - Treat all files below mount point as executable.
ihash       - Always fake inode numbers rather than using the ones returned
            by the filesystem.  This allows to use broken filesystems which
            don't return unambiguous inode numbers, even if they are not
            recognized as such by Cygwin.
noacl       - Cygwin ignores filesystem ACLs and only fakes a subset of
            permission bits based on the DOS readonly attribute.  This
            behaviour is the default on FAT and FAT32.  The flag is
            ignored on NFS filesystems.
nosuid      - No suid files are allowed (currently unimplemented).
notexec     - Treat all files below mount point as not executable.
nouser      - Mount is a system-wide mount.
override    - Force the override of an immutable mount point (currently "/").
posix=0     - Switch off case sensitivity for paths under this mount point
            (default for the cygdrive prefix).
posix=1     - Switch on case sensitivity for paths under this mount point
            (default for all other mount points).
sparse      - Switch on support for sparse files.  This option only makes
               sense on NTFS and then only if you really need sparse files.
            Cygwin does not try to create sparse files by default for
            performance reasons.
text        - Files default to CRLF text mode line endings.
user        - Mount is a user mount.
```

While normally the execute permission bits are used to evaluate executability, this is not possible on filesystems which don't support permissions at all (like FAT/FAT32), or if ACLs are ignored on filesystems supporting them (see the aforementioned acl mount option). In these cases, the following heuristic is used to evaluate if a file is executable: Files ending in certain extensions (.exe, .com, .lnk) are assumed to be executable. Files whose first two characters are "#!", "MZ", or ":\n" are also considered to be executable. The `exec` option is used to instruct Cygwin that the mounted file is "executable". If the `exec` option is used with a directory then all files in the directory are executable. This option allows other files to be marked as executable and avoids the overhead of opening each file to check for "magic" bytes. The `cygexec` option is very similar to `exec`, but also prevents Cygwin from setting up commands and environment variables for a normal Windows program, adding another small performance gain. The opposite of these options is the `notexec` option, which means that no files should be marked as executable under that mount point.

A correct root directory is quite essential to the operation of Cygwin. A default root directory is evaluated at startup so a `fstab` entry for the root directory is not necessary. If it's wrong, nothing will work as expected. Therefore, the root directory evaluated by Cygwin itself is treated as an immutable mount point and can't be overridden in /etc/fstab... unless you think you really know what you're doing. In this case, use the `override` flag in the options field in the `/etc/fstab` file. Since this is a dangerous thing to do, do so at your own risk.

`/usr/bin` and `/usr/lib` are by default also automatic mount points generated by the Cygwin DLL similar to the way the root directory is evaluated. `/usr/bin` points to the directory the Cygwin DLL is installed in, `/usr/lib` is supposed to point to the `/lib` directory. This choice is safe and usually shouldn't be changed. An fstab entry for them is not required.

`nouser` mount points are not overridable by a later call to **mount**. Mount points given in `/etc/fstab` are by default `nouser` mount points, unless you specify the option `user`. This allows the administrator to set certain paths so that they are not overridable by users. In contrast, all mount points in the user specific fstab file are `user` mount points.

The fifth and sixth field are ignored. They are so far only specified to keep a Linux-like fstab file layout.

Note that you don't have to specify an fstab entry for the root dir, unless you want to have the root dir pointing to somewhere entirely different (hopefully you know what you're doing), or if you want to mount the root dir with special options (for instance, as text mount).

Example entries:

- Just a normal mount point:

  ```
  c:/foo /bar fat32 binary 0 0
  ```

- A mount point for a textmode mount with case sensitivity switched off:

  ```
  C:/foo /bar/baz ntfs text,posix=0 0 0
  ```

- A mount point for a Windows directory with spaces in it:

  ```
  C:/Documents\040and\040Settings /docs ext3 binary 0 0
  ```

- A mount point for a remote directory, don't store POSIX permissions in ACLs:

  ```
  //server/share/subdir /srv/subdir smbfs binary,noacl 0 0
  ```

- This is just a comment:

  ```
  # This is just a comment
  ```

- Set the cygdrive prefix to /mnt:

  ```
  none /mnt cygdrive binary 0 0
  ```

- Remount /var to /usr/var:

  ```
  /var /usr/var none bind
  ```

  Assuming `/var` points to `C:/cygwin/var`, `/usr/var` now also points to `C:/cygwin/var`. This is equivalent to the Linux `bind` option available since Linux 2.4.0.

Whenever Cygwin generates a Win32 path from a POSIX one, it uses the longest matching prefix in the mount table. Thus, if `C:` is mounted as `/c` and also as `/`, then Cygwin would translate `C:/foo/bar` to `/c/foo/bar`. This translation is normally only used when trying to derive the POSIX equivalent current directory. Otherwise, the handling of MS-DOS filenames bypasses the mount table.

If you want to see the current set of mount points valid in your session, you can invoke the Cygwin tool **mount** without arguments:

Example 3.1 Displaying the current set of mount points

```
bash$ mount
f:/cygwin/bin on /usr/bin type ntfs (binary,auto)
f:/cygwin/lib on /usr/lib type ntfs (binary,auto)
f:/cygwin on / type ntfs (binary,auto)
e:/src on /usr/src type vfat (binary)
c: on /cygdrive/c type ntfs (binary,posix=0,user,noumount,auto)
e: on /cygdrive/e type vfat (binary,posix=0,user,noumount,auto)
```

You can also use the **mount** command to add new mount points, and the **umount** to delete them. However, since they are only stored in memory, these mount points will disappear as soon as your last Cygwin process ends. See mount(1) and umount(1) for more information.

3.1.3 UNC paths

Apart from the unified POSIX tree starting at the / directory, UNC pathnames starting with two slashes and a server name (//machine/share/...) are supported as well. They are handled as POSIX paths if only containing forward slashes. There's also a virtual directory // which allows to enumerate the fileservers known to the local machine with **ls**. Same goes for the UNC paths of the type //machine, which allow to enumerate the shares provided by the server machine. For often used UNC paths it makes sense to add them to the mount table (see Section 3.1.2 so they are included in the unified POSIX path tree.

3.1.4 The cygdrive path prefix

As already outlined in Section 1.6.3, you can access arbitary drives on your system by using the cygdrive path prefix. The default value for this prefix is /cygdrive, and a path to any drive can be constructed by using the cygdrive prefix and appending the drive letter as subdirectory, like this:

```
bash$ ls -l /cygdrive/f/somedir
```

This lists the content of the directory F:\somedir.

The cygdrive prefix is a virtual directory under which all drives on a system are subsumed. The mount options of the cygdrive prefix is used for all file access through the cygdrive prefixed drives. For instance, assuming the cygdrive mount options are binary,posix=0, then any file /cygdrive/x/file will be opened in binary mode by default (mount option binary), and the case of the filename doesn't matter (mount option posix=0).

The cygdrive prefix flags are also used for all UNC paths starting with two slashes, unless they are accessed through a mount point. For instance, consider these /etc/fstab entries:

```
//server/share /mysrv    ntfs     posix=1,acl  0 0
none           /cygdrive cygdrive posix=0,noacl 0 0
```

Assume there's a file \\server\share\foo on the share. When accessing it as /mysrv/foo, then the flags posix=1,acl of the /mysrv mount point are used. When accessing it as //server/share/foo, then the flags for the cygdrive prefix, posix=0,noacl are used.

Note

This only applies to UNC paths using forward slashes. When using backslashes the flags for native paths are used. See Section 3.1.7.

The cygdrive prefix may be changed in the fstab file as outlined above. Please note that you must not use the cygdrive prefix for any other mount point. For instance this:

```
none /cygdrive cygdrive binary 0 0
D:   /cygdrive/d somefs text 0 0
```

will not make file access using the /mnt/d path prefix suddenly using textmode. If you want to mount any drive explicitly in another mode than the cygdrive prefix, use a distinct path prefix:

```
none /cygdrive cygdrive binary 0 0
D:   /mnt/d somefs text 0 0
```

To simplify scripting, Cygwin also provides a /proc/cygdrive symlink, which allows to use a fixed path in scripts, even if the actual cygdrive prefix has been changed, or is different between different users. So, in scripts, conveniently use the /proc/cygdrive symlink to successfully access files independently from the current cygdrive prefix:

```
$ mount -p
Prefix              Type        Flags
/mnt                user        binmode
$ cat > x.sh <<EOF
cd /proc/cygdrive/c/Windows/System32/Drivers/etc
ls -l hosts
EOF
$ sh -c ./x.sh
-rwxrwx---+ 1 SYSTEM SYSTEM 826 Sep  4 22:43 hosts
```

3.1.5 The usertemp file system type

On Windows, the environment variable TEMP specifies the location of the temp folder. It serves the same purpose as the /tmp/ directory in Unix systems. In contrast to /tmp/, it is by default a different folder for every Windows. By using the special purpose usertemp file system, that temp folder can be mapped to /tmp/. This is particularly useful in setups where the administrator wants to write-protect the entire Cygwin directory. The usertemp file system can be configured in /etc/fstab like this:

```
none /tmp usertemp binary,posix=0 0 0
```

3.1.6 Symbolic links

Symbolic links are not present and supported on Windows until Windows Vista/Server 2008, and then only on some filesystems. Since POSIX applications are rightfully expecting to use symlinks and the symlink(2) system call, Cygwin had to find a workaround for this Windows flaw.

Cygwin creates symbolic links potentially in multiple different ways:

- The default symlinks are plain files containing a magic cookie followed by the path to which the link points. They are marked with the DOS SYSTEM attribute so that only files with that attribute have to be read to determine whether or not the file is a symbolic link.

Note

Starting with Cygwin 1.7, symbolic links are using UTF-16 to encode the filename of the target file, to better support internationalization. Symlinks created by older Cygwin releases can be read just fine. However, you could run into problems with them if you're now using another character set than the one you used when creating these symlinks (see Section 2.4.4). Please note that this new UTF-16 style of symlinks is not compatible with older Cygwin release, which can't read the target filename correctly.

- The shortcut style symlinks are Windows .lnk shortcut files with a special header and the DOS READONLY attribute set. This symlink type is created if the environment variable CYGWIN (see Section 3.5) is set to contain the string winsymlinks or winsymlinks:lnk. On the MVFS filesystem, which does not support the DOS SYSTEM attribute, this is the one and only supported symlink type, independently from the winsymlinks setting.

- Native Windows symlinks are only created on Windows Vista/2008 and later, and only on filesystems supporting reparse points. Due to to their weird restrictions and behaviour, they are only created if the user explicitly requests creating them. This is done by setting the environment variable `CYGWIN` to contain the string `winsymlinks:native` or `winsymlinks:nativestrict`. For the difference between these two settings, see Section 3.5. On AFS, native symlinks are the only supported type of symlink due to AFS lacking support for DOS attributes. This is independent from the `winsymlinks` setting.

  Creation of native symlinks follows special rules to ensure the links are usable outside of Cygwin. This includes dereferencing any Cygwin-only symlinks that lie in the target path.

- On the NFS filesystem, Cygwin always creates real NFS symlinks.

All of the above four symlink types are recognized and used as symlinks under all circumstances. However, if the default plain file symlink type is lacking its DOS SYSTEM bit, or if the shortcut file is lacking the DOS READONLY attribute, they are not recognized as symlink.

Apart from these four types, there's also a fifth type, which is recognized as symlink but never generated by Cygwin, directory junctions. This is an older reparse point type, supported by Windows since Windows 2000. Filesystem junctions on the other hand are not handled as symlinks, since otherwise they would not be recognized as filesystem borders by commands like **find -xdev**.

3.1.7 Using native Win32 paths

Using native Win32 paths in Cygwin, while possible, is generally inadvisable. Those paths circumvent all internal integrity checking and bypass the information given in the Cygwin mount table.

The following paths are treated as native Win32 paths in Cygwin:

- All paths starting with a drive specifier

  ```
  C:\foo
  C:/foo
  ```

- All paths containing at least one backslash as path component

  ```
  C:/foo/bar\baz/...
  ```

- UNC paths using backslashes

  ```
  \\server\share\...
  ```

When accessing files using native Win32 paths as above, Cygwin uses a default setting for the mount flags. All paths using DOS notation will be treated as case insensitive, and permissions are just faked as if the underlying drive is a FAT drive. This also applies to NTFS and other filesystems which usually are capable of case sensitivity and storing permissions.

3.1.8 Using the Win32 file API in Cygwin applications

Special care must be taken if your application uses Win32 file API functions like `CreateFile` to access files using relative pathnames, or if your application uses functions like `CreateProcess` or `ShellExecute` to start other applications.

When a Cygwin application is started, the Windows idea of the current working directory (CWD) is not necessarily the same as the Cygwin CWD. There are a couple of restrictions in the Win32 API, which disallow certain directories as Win32 CWD:

- The Windows subsystem only supports CWD paths of up to 258 chars. This restriction doesn't apply for Cygwin processes, at least not as long as they use the POSIX API (chdir, getcwd). This means, if a Cygwin process has a CWD using an absolute path longer than 258 characters, the Cygwin CWD and the Windows CWD differ.

- The Win32 API call to set the current directory, `SetCurrentDirectory`, fails for directories for which the user has no permissions, even if the user is an administrator. This restriction doesn't apply for Cygwin processes, if they are running under an administrator account.

- `SetCurrentDirectory` does not support case-sensitive filenames.

- Last, but not least, `SetCurrentDirectory` can't work on virtual Cygwin paths like /proc or /cygdrive. These paths only exists in the Cygwin realm so they have no meaning to a native Win32 process.

As long as the Cygwin CWD is usable as Windows CWD, the Cygwin and Windows CWDs are in sync within a process. However, if the Cygwin process changes its working directory into one of the directories which are unusable as Windows CWD, we're in trouble. If the process uses the Win32 API to access a file using a relative pathname, the resulting absolute path would not match the expectations of the process. In the worst case, the wrong files are deleted.

To workaround this problem, Cygwin sets the Windows CWD to a special directory in this case. This special directory points to a virtual filesystem within the native NT namespace (`\??\PIPE\`). Since it's not a real filesystem, the deliberate effect is that a call to, for instance, `CreateFile ("foo", ...);` will fail, as long as the processes CWD doesn't work as Windows CWD.

So, in general, don't use the Win32 file API in Cygwin applications. If you **really** need to access files using the Win32 API, or if you **really** have to use `CreateProcess` to start applications, rather than the POSIX `exec(3)` family of functions, you have to make sure that the Cygwin CWD is set to some directory which is valid as Win32 CWD.

3.1.9   Additional Path-related Information

The **cygpath** program provides the ability to translate between Win32 and POSIX pathnames in shell scripts. See cygpath(1) for the details.

The `HOME`, `PATH`, and `LD_LIBRARY_PATH` environment variables are automatically converted from Win32 format to POSIX format (e.g. from `c:/cygwin\bin` to `/bin`, if there was a mount from that Win32 path to that POSIX path) when a Cygwin process first starts.

Symbolic links can also be used to map Win32 pathnames to POSIX. For example, the command **ln -s //pollux/home/joe/data /data** would have about the same effect as creating a mount point from `//pollux/home/joe/data` to `/data` using **mount**, except that symbolic links cannot set the default file access mode. Other differences are that the mapping is distributed throughout the file system and proceeds by iteratively walking the directory tree instead of matching the longest prefix in a kernel table. Note that symbolic links will only work on network drives that are properly configured to support the "system" file attribute. Many do not do so by default (the Unix Samba server does not by default, for example).

3.2   Text and Binary modes

3.2.1   The Issue

On a UNIX system, when an application reads from a file it gets exactly what's in the file on disk and the converse is true for writing. The situation is different in the DOS/Windows world where a file can be opened in one of two modes, binary or text. In the binary mode the system behaves exactly as in UNIX. However on writing in text mode, a NL (\n, ^J) is transformed into the sequence CR (\r, ^M) NL.

This can wreak havoc with the seek/fseek calls since the number of bytes actually in the file may differ from that seen by the application.

The mode can be specified explicitly as explained in the Programming section below. In an ideal DOS/Windows world, all programs using lines as records (such as **bash**, **make**, **sed** ...) would open files (and change the mode of their standard input and output) as text. All other programs (such as **cat**, **cmp**, **tr** ...) would use binary mode. In practice with Cygwin, programs that deal explicitly with object files specify binary mode (this is the case of **od**, which is helpful to diagnose CR problems). Most other programs (such as **sed**, **cmp**, **tr**) use the default mode.

3.2.2   The default Cygwin behavior

The Cygwin system gives us some flexibility in deciding how files are to be opened when the mode is not specified explicitly. The rules are evolving, this section gives the design goals.

a. If the filename is specified as a POSIX path and it appears to reside on a file system that is mounted (i.e. if its pathname starts with a directory displayed by **mount**), then the default is specified by the mount flag. If the file is a symbolic link, the mode of the target file system applies.

b. If the file is specified via a MS-DOS pathname (i.e., it contains a backslash or a colon), the default is binary.

c. Pipes, sockets and non-file devices are opened in binary mode. For pipes opened through the pipe() system call you can use the setmode() function (see Section 3.2.4 to switch to textmode. For pipes opened through popen(), you can simply specify text or binary mode just like in calls to fopen().

d. Sockets and other non-file devices are always opened in binary mode.

e. When redirecting, the Cygwin shells uses rules (a-d). Non-Cygwin shells always pipe and redirect with binary mode. With non-Cygwin shells the commands **cat filename | program** and **program < filename** are not equivalent when `filename` is on a text-mounted partition.

   The programs **u2d** and **d2u** can be used to add or remove CR's from a file. **u2d** add's CR's before a NL. **d2u** removes CR's. Use the --help option to these commands for more information.

3.2.3   Binary or text?

UNIX programs that have been written for maximum portability will know the difference between text and binary files and act appropriately under Cygwin. Most programs included in the official Cygwin distributions should work well in the default mode.

Binmode is the best choice usually since it's faster and easier to handle, unless you want to exchange files with native Win32 applications. It makes most sense to keep the Cygwin distribution and your Cygwin home directory in binmode and generate text files in binmode (with UNIX LF lineendings). Most Windows applications can handle binmode files just fine. A notable exception is the mini-editor **Notepad**, which handles UNIX lineendings incorrectly and only produces output files with DOS CRLF lineendings.

You can convert files between CRLF and LF lineendings by using certain tools in the Cygwin distribution like **d2u** and **u2d** from the cygutils package. You can also specify a directory in the mount table to be mounted in textmode so you can use that directory for exchange purposes.

As application programmer you can decide on a file by file base, or you can specify default open modes depending on the purpose for which the application open files. See the next section for a description of your choices.

3.2.4   Programming

In the `open()` function call, binary mode can be specified with the flag `O_BINARY` and text mode with `O_TEXT`. These symbols are defined in `fcntl.h`.

The `mkstemp()` and `mkstemps()` calls force binary mode. Use `mkostemp()` or `mkostemps()` with the same flags as `open()` for more control on temporary files.

In the `fopen()` and `popen()` function calls, binary mode can be specified by adding a `b` to the mode string. Text mode is specified by adding a `t` to the mode string.

The mode of a file can be changed by the call `setmode(fd, mode)` where `fd` is a file descriptor (an integer) and `mode` is `O_BINARY` or `O_TEXT`. The function returns `O_BINARY` or `O_TEXT` depending on the mode before the call, and `EOF` on error.

There's also a convenient way to set the default open modes used in an application by just linking against various object files provided by Cygwin. For instance, if you want to make sure that all files are always opened in binary mode by an application, regardless of the mode of the underlying mount point, just add the file `/lib/binmode.o` to the link stage of the application in your project, like this:

```
$ gcc my_tiny_app.c /lib/binmode.o -o my_tiny_app
```

Starting with Cygwin 1.7.7, you can use the even simpler:

```
$ gcc my_tiny_app.c -lbinmode -o my_tiny_app
```

This adds code which sets the default open mode for all files opened by **my_tiny_app** to binary for reading and writing.

Cygwin provides the following libraries and object files to set the default open mode just by linking an application against them:

-
```
/lib/libautomode.a       -  Open files for reading in textmode,
/lib/automode.o             open files for writing in binary mode
```

-
```
/lib/libbinmode.a        -  Open files for reading and writing in binary mode
/lib/binmode.o
```

-
```
/lib/libtextmode.a       -  Open files for reading and writing in textmode
/lib/textmode.o
```

-
```
/lib/libtextreadmode.a   -  Open files for reading in textmode,
/lib/textreadmode.o         keep default behaviour for writing.
```

3.3 File permissions

On FAT or FAT32 filesystems, files are always readable, and Cygwin uses the DOS read-only attribute to determine if they are writable. Files are considered to be executable if the filename ends with .bat, .com or .exe, or if its content starts with #!. Consequently **chmod** can only affect the "w" mode, it silently ignores actions involving the other modes. This means that **ls -l** needs to open and read files. It can thus be relatively slow.

On NTFS, file permissions are evaluated using the Access Control Lists (ACLs) attached to a file. This can be switched off by using the "noacl" option to the respective mount point in the `/etc/fstab` or `/etc/fstab.d/$USER` file. For more information on file permissions, see Section 3.6.

On NFS shares, file permissions are exactly the POSIX permissions transmitted from the server using the NFSv3 protocol, if the NFS client is the one from Microsoft's "Services For Unix", or the one built into Windows Vista or later.

Only the user and group ownership is not necessarily correct.

3.4 Special filenames

3.4.1 Special files in /etc

Certain files in Cygwin's `/etc` directory are read by Cygwin before the mount table has been established. The list of files is

```
/etc/fstab
/etc/fstab.d/$USER
/etc/passwd
/etc/group
```

These file are read using native Windows NT functions which have no notion of Cygwin symlinks or POSIX paths. For that reason there are a few requirements as far as `/etc` is concerned.

To access these files, the Cygwin DLL evaluates it's own full Windows path, strips off the innermost directory component and adds "\etc". Let's assume the Cygwin DLL is installed as `C:\cygwin\bin\cygwin1.dll`. First the DLL name as well as the innermost directory (`bin`) is stripped off: `C:\cygwin\`. Then "etc" and the filename to look for is attached: `C:\cygwin\etc\fstab`. So the /etc directory must be parallel to the directory in which the cygwin1.dll exists and `/etc` must not be a Cygwin symlink pointing to another directory. Consequentially none of the files from the above list, including the directory `/etc/fstab.d` is allowed to be a Cygwin symlink either.

However, native NTFS symlinks and reparse points are transparent when accessing the above files so all these files as well as `/etc` itself may be NTFS symlinks or reparse points.

Last but not least, make sure that these files are world-readable. Every process of any user account has to read these files potentially, so world-readability is essential. The only exception are the user specific files `/etc/fstab.d/$USER`, which only have to be readable by the $USER user account itself.

3.4.2   Invalid filenames

Filenames invalid under Win32 are not necessarily invalid under Cygwin since release 1.7.0. There are a few rules which apply to Windows filenames. Most notably, DOS device names like AUX, COM1, LPT1 or PRN (to name a few) cannot be used as filename or extension in a native Win32 application. So filenames like prn.txt or foo.aux are invalid filenames for native Win32 applications.

This restriction doesn't apply to Cygwin applications. Cygwin can create and access files with such names just fine. Just don't try to use these files with native Win32 applications.

3.4.3   Forbidden characters in filenames

Some characters are disallowed in filenames on Windows filesystems. These forbidden characters are the ASCII control characters from ASCII value 1 to 31, plus the following characters which have a special meaning in the Win32 API:

```
"   *   :   <   >   ?   |   \
```

Cygwin can't fix this, but it has a method to workaround this restriction. All of the above characters, except for the backslash, are converted to special UNICODE characters in the range 0xf000 to 0xf0ff (the "Private use area") when creating or accessing files.

The backslash has to be exempt from this conversion, because Cygwin accepts Win32 filenames including backslashes as path separators on input. Converting backslashes using the above method would make this impossible.

Additionally Win32 filenames can't contain trailing dots and spaces for DOS backward compatibility. When trying to create files with trailing dots or spaces, all of them are removed before the file is created. This restriction only affects native Win32 applications. Cygwin applications can create and access files with trailing dots and spaces without problems.

An exception from this rule are some network filesystems (NetApp, NWFS) which choke on these filenames. They return with an error like "No such file or directory" when trying to create such files. Starting with Cygwin 1.7.6, Cygwin recognizes these filesystems and works around this problem by applying the same rule as for the other forbidden characters. Leading spaces and trailing dots and spaces will be converted to UNICODE characters in the private use area. This behaviour can be switched on explicitly for a filesystem or a directory tree by using the mount option dos.

3.4.4   Filenames with unusual (foreign) characters

Windows filesystems use Unicode encoded as UTF-16 to store filename information. If you don't use the UTF-8 character set (see Section 2.4) then there's a chance that a filename is using one or more characters which have no representation in the character set you're using.

Note

In the default "C" locale, Cygwin creates filenames using the UTF-8 charset. This will always result in some valid filename by default, but again might impose problems when switching to a non-"C" or non-"UTF-8" charset.

Note

To avoid this scenario altogether, always use UTF-8 as the character set.

If you don't want or can't use UTF-8 as character set for whatever reason, you will nevertheless be able to access the file. How does that work? When Cygwin converts the filename from UTF-16 to your character set, it recognizes characters which can't be converted. If that occurs, Cygwin replaces the non-convertible character with a special character sequence. The sequence starts with an ASCII CAN character (hex code 0x18, equivalent Control-X), followed by the UTF-8 representation of the character. The result is a filename containing some ugly looking characters. While it doesn't **look** nice, it **is** nice, because Cygwin knows how to convert this filename back to UTF-16. The filename will be converted using your usual character set. However, when Cygwin recognizes an ASCII CAN character, it skips over the ASCII CAN and handles the following bytes as a UTF-8 character. Thus, the filename is symmetrically converted back to UTF-16 and you can access the file.

Note

Please be aware that this method is not entirely foolproof. In some character set combinations it might not work for certain native characters.

Only by using the UTF-8 charset you can avoid this problem safely.

3.4.5 Case sensitive filenames

In the Win32 subsystem filenames are only case-preserved, but not case-sensitive. You can't access two files in the same directory which only differ by case, like `Abc` and `aBc`. While NTFS (and some remote filesystems) support case-sensitivity, the NT kernel starting with Windows XP does not support it by default. Rather, you have to tweak a registry setting and reboot. For that reason, case-sensitivity can not be supported by Cygwin, unless you change that registry value.

If you really want case-sensitivity in Cygwin, you can switch it on by setting the registry value

`HKLM\SYSTEM\CurrentControlSet\Control\Session Manager\kernel\obcaseinsensitive`

to 0 and reboot the machine.

Note

When installing Microsoft's Services For Unix (SFU), you're asked if you want to use case-sensitive filenames. If you answer "yes" at this point, the installer will change the aforementioned registry value to 0, too. So, if you have SFU installed, there's some chance that the registry value is already set to case sensitivity.

After you set this registry value to 0, Cygwin will be case-sensitive by default on NTFS and NFS filesystems. However, there are limitations: while two **programs** `Abc.exe` and `aBc.exe` can be created and accessed like other files, starting applications is still case-insensitive due to Windows limitations and so the program you try to launch may not be the one actually started. Also, be aware that using two filenames which only differ by case might result in some weird interoperability issues with native Win32 applications. You're using case-sensitivity at your own risk. You have been warned!

Even if you use case-sensitivity, it might be feasible to switch to case-insensitivity for certain paths for better interoperability with native Win32 applications (even if it's just Windows Explorer). You can do this on a per-mount point base, by using the "posix=0" mount option in `/etc/fstab`, or your `/etc/fstab.d/$USER` file.

`/cygdrive` paths are case-insensitive by default. The reason is that the native Windows %PATH% environment variable is not always using the correct case for all paths in it. As a result, if you use case-sensitivity on the `/cygdrive` prefix, your shell might claim that it can't find Windows commands like **attrib** or **net**. To ease the pain, the `/cygdrive` path is case-insensitive by default and you have to use the "posix=1" setting explicitly in `/etc/fstab` or `/etc/fstab.d/$USER` to switch it to case-sensitivity, or you have to make sure that the native Win32 %PATH% environment variable is using the correct case for all paths throughout.

Note that mount points as well as device names and virtual paths like /proc are always case-sensitive! The only exception are the subdirectories and filenames under /proc/registry, /proc/registry32 and /proc/registry64. Registry access is always case-insensitive. Read on for more information.

3.4.6 POSIX devices

While there is no need to create a POSIX `/dev` directory, the directory is automatically created as part of a Cygwin installation. It's existence is often a prerequisit to run certain applications which create symbolic links, fifos, or UNIX sockets in `/dev`. Also, the directories `/dev/shm` and `/dev/mqueue` are required to exist to use named POSIX semaphores, shared memory, and message queues, so a system without a real `/dev` directory is functionally crippled.

Apart from that, Cygwin automatically simulates POSIX devices internally. Up to Cygwin 1.7.11, these devices couldn't be seen with the command **ls /dev/** although commands such as **ls /dev/tty** worked fine. Starting with Cygwin 1.7.12, the `/dev` directory is automagically populated with existing POSIX devices by Cygwin in a way comparable with a udev based virtual `/dev` directory under Linux.

Cygwin supports the following character devices commonly found on POSIX systems:

```
/dev/null
/dev/zero
/dev/full

/dev/console  Pseudo device name for the current console window of a session.
    Up to Cygwin 1.7.9, this was the only name for a console.
    Different consoles were indistinguishable.
    Cygwin's /dev/console is not quite comparable with the console
    device on UNIX machines.

/dev/cons0        Starting with Cygwin 1.7.10, Console sessions are numbered from
/dev/cons1  /dev/cons0 upwards.  Console device names are pseudo device
...   names, only accessible from processes within this very console
    session.  This is due to a restriction in Windows.

/dev/tty  The current controlling tty of a session.

/dev/ptmx Pseudo tty master device.

/dev/pty0 Pseudo ttys are numbered from /dev/pty0 upwards as they are
/dev/pty1 requested.
...

/dev/ttyS0  Serial communication devices.  ttyS0 == Win32 COM1,
/dev/ttyS1  ttyS1 == COM2, etc.
...

/dev/pipe
/dev/fifo

/dev/kmsg Kernel message pipe, for usage with sys logger services.

/dev/random Random number generator.
/dev/urandom

/dev/dsp  Default sound device of the system.
```

Cygwin also has several Windows-specific devices:

```
/dev/com1 The serial ports, starting with COM1 which is the same as ttyS0.
/dev/com2 Please use /dev/ttySx instead.
...

/dev/conin  Same as Windows CONIN$.
/dev/conout Same as Windows CONOUT$.
/dev/clipboard  The Windows clipboard, text only
/dev/windows  The Windows message queue.
```

Block devices are accessible by Cygwin processes using fixed POSIX device names. These POSIX device names are generated using a direct conversion from the POSIX namespace to the internal NT namespace. E.g. the first harddisk is the NT internal device \device\harddisk0\partition0 or the first partition on the third harddisk is \device\harddisk2\partition1. The first floppy in the system is \device\floppy0, the first CD-ROM is \device\cdrom0 and the first tape drive is \device\tape0.

The mapping from physical device to the name of the device in the internal NT namespace can be found in various places. For hard disks and CD/DVD drives, the Windows "Disk Management" utility (part of the "Computer Management" console) shows that the mapping of "Disk 0" is \device\harddisk0. "CD-ROM 2" is \device\cdrom2. Another place to find this mapping is the "Device Management" console. Disks have a "Location" number, tapes have a "Tape Symbolic Name", etc. Unfortunately, the places where this information is found is not very well-defined.

For external disks (USB-drives, CF-cards in a cardreader, etc) you can use Cygwin to show the mapping. /proc/partitions contains a list of raw drives known to Cygwin. The **df** command shows a list of drives and their respective sizes. If you match the information between `/proc/partitions` and the **df** output, you should be able to figure out which external drive corresponds to which raw disk device name.

Note

Apart from tape devices which are not block devices and are by default accessed directly, accessing mass storage devices raw is something you should only do if you know what you're doing and know how to handle the information. **Writing** to a raw mass storage device you should only do if you **really** know what you're doing and are aware of the fact that any mistake can destroy important information, for the device, and for you. So, please, handle this ability with care. **You have been warned.**

Last but not least, the mapping from POSIX /dev namespace to internal NT namespace is as follows:

```
POSIX device name       Internal NT device name

/dev/st0           \device\tape0, rewind
/dev/nst0          \device\tape0, no-rewind
/dev/st1           \device\tape1
/dev/nst1          \device\tape1
...
/dev/st15
/dev/nst15

/dev/fd0           \device\floppy0
/dev/fd1           \device\floppy1
...
/dev/fd15

/dev/sr0           \device\cdrom0
/dev/sr1           \device\cdrom1
...
/dev/sr15

/dev/scd0          \device\cdrom0
/dev/scd1          \device\cdrom1
...
/dev/scd15

/dev/sda           \device\harddisk0\partition0   (whole disk)
/dev/sda1          \device\harddisk0\partition1   (first partition)
...
/dev/sda15          \device\harddisk0\partition15 (fifteenth partition)

/dev/sdb           \device\harddisk1\partition0
/dev/sdb1          \device\harddisk1\partition1

[up to]

/dev/sddx          \device\harddisk127\partition0
/dev/sddx1          \device\harddisk127\partition1
...
/dev/sddx15          \device\harddisk127\partition15
```

if you don't like these device names, feel free to create symbolic links as they are created on Linux systems for convenience:

```
ln -s /dev/sr0 /dev/cdrom
ln -s /dev/nst0 /dev/tape
...
```

3.4.7   The .exe extension

Win32 executable filenames end with .exe but the .exe need not be included in the command, so that traditional UNIX names can be used. However, for programs that end in .bat and .com, you cannot omit the extension.

As a side effect, the **ls filename** gives information about filename.exe if filename.exe exists and filename does not. In the same situation the function call stat("filename",..) gives information about filename.exe. The two files can be distinguished by examining their inodes, as demonstrated below.

```
bash$ ls *
a        a.exe      b.exe
bash$ ls -i a a.exe
445885548 a          435996602 a.exe
bash$ ls -i b b.exe
432961010 b          432961010 b.exe
```

If a shell script myprog and a program myprog.exe coexist in a directory, the shell script has precedence and is selected for execution of **myprog**. Note that this was quite the reverse up to Cygwin 1.5.19. It has been changed for consistency with the rest of Cygwin.

The **gcc** compiler produces an executable named filename.exe when asked to produce filename. This allows many makefiles written for UNIX systems to work well under Cygwin.

3.4.8   The /proc filesystem

Cygwin, like Linux and other similar operating systems, supports the /proc virtual filesystem. The files in this directory are representations of various aspects of your system, for example the command **cat /proc/cpuinfo** displays information such as what model and speed processor you have.

One unique aspect of the Cygwin /proc filesystem is /proc/registry, see next section.

The Cygwin /proc is not as complete as the one in Linux, but it provides significant capabilities. The procps package contains several utilities that use it.

3.4.9   The /proc/registry filesystem

The /proc/registry filesystem provides read-only access to the Windows registry. It displays each KEY as a directory and each VALUE as a file. As anytime you deal with the Windows registry, use caution since changes may result in an unstable or broken system. There are additionally subdirectories called /proc/registry32 and /proc/registry64. They are identical to /proc/registry on 32 bit host OSes. On 64 bit host OSes, /proc/registry32 opens the 32 bit processes view on the registry, while /proc/registry64 opens the 64 bit processes view.

Reserved characters ('/', '\', ':', and '%') or reserved names (. and ..) are converted by percent-encoding:

```
bash$ regtool list -v '\HKEY_LOCAL_MACHINE\SYSTEM\MountedDevices'
...
\DosDevices\C: (REG_BINARY) = cf a8 97 e8 00 08 fe f7
...
bash$ cd /proc/registry/HKEY_LOCAL_MACHINE/SYSTEM
bash$ ls -l MountedDevices
...
-r--r----- 1 Admin SYSTEM  12 Dec 10 11:20 %5CDosDevices%5CC%3A
...
bash$ od -t x1 MountedDevices/%5CDosDevices%5CC%3A
0000000 cf a8 97 e8 00 08 fe f7 01 00 00 00
```

The unnamed (default) value of a key can be accessed using the filename @.

If a registry key contains a subkey and a value with the same name foo, Cygwin displays the subkey as foo and the value as foo%val.

3.4.10   The @pathnames

To circumvent the limitations on shell line length in the native Windows command shells, Cygwin programs, when invoked by non-Cygwin processes, expand their arguments starting with "@" in a special way. If a file `pathname` exists, the argument `@pathname` expands recursively to the content of `pathname`. Double quotes can be used inside the file to delimit strings containing blank space. In the following example compare the behaviors **/bin/echo** when run from bash and from the Windows command prompt.

Example 3.2 Using @pathname

```
bash$ /bin/echo 'This   is   "a      long" line' > mylist
bash$ /bin/echo @mylist
@mylist
bash$ cmd
c:\> c:\cygwin\bin\echo @mylist
This is a      long line
```

3.5   The `CYGWIN` environment variable

3.5.1   Implemented options

The `CYGWIN` environment variable is used to configure many global settings for the Cygwin runtime system. It contains the options listed below, separated by blank characters. Many options can be turned off by prefixing with `no`.

- `(no)detect_bloda` - If set, Cygwin will try to detect foreign applications which try to inject threads into a Cygwin process, or which redirect system sockets by providing an enforced so-called `Layered Service Provider`. This may or may not help to detect BLODAs. Don't use this option for day-to-day usage, it will slow down every thread and socket creation!

- `(no)dosfilewarning` - If set, Cygwin will warn the first time a user uses an "MS-DOS" style path name rather than a POSIX-style path name. Defaults to off.

- `(no)export` - If set, the final values of these settings are re-exported to the environment as `CYGWIN` again. Defaults to off.

- `error_start:Win32filepath` - if set, runs `Win32filepath` when cygwin encounters a fatal error, which is useful for debugging. `Win32filepath` is usually set to the path to **gdb** or **dumper**, for example `C:\cygwin\bin\gdb.exe`. There is no default set.

- `(no)glob[:ignorecase]` - if set, command line arguments containing UNIX-style file wildcard characters (brackets, braces, question mark, asterisk, escaped with \\) are expanded into lists of files that match those wildcards. This is applicable only to programs run from non-Cygwin programs such as a CMD prompt. That means that this setting does not affect globbing operations for shells such as bash, sh, tcsh, zsh, etc. Default is set.

  This option also accepts an optional `[no]ignorecase` modifer. If supplied, wildcard matching is case insensitive. The default is `noignorecase`

- `(no)pipe_byte` - causes Cygwin to open pipes in byte mode rather than message mode.

- `proc_retry:n` - causes `fork()` and `exec*()` to retry n times when a child process fails due to certain windows-specific errors. These errors usually occur when processes are being started while a user is logging off.

- `(no)reset_com` - if set, serial ports are reset to 9600-8-N-1 with no flow control when used. This is done at open time and when handles are inherited. Defaults to set.

- `(no)wincmdln` - if set, the windows complete command line (truncated to ~32K) will be passed on any processes that it creates in addition to the normal UNIX argv list. Defaults to not set.

- winsymlinks:{lnk,native,nativestrict} - if set to just winsymlinks or winsymlinks:lnk, Cygwin creates symlinks as Windows shortcuts with a special header and the R/O attribute set.

  If set to winsymlinks:native or winsymlinks:nativestrict, Cygwin creates symlinks as native Windows symlinks on filesystems and OS versions supporting them. If the OS is known not to support native symlinks (Windows XP, Windows Server 2003), a warning message is produced once per session.

  The difference between winsymlinks:native and winsymlinks:nativestrict is this: If the filesystem supports native symlinks and Cygwin fails to create a native symlink for some reason, it will fall back to creating Cygwin default symlinks with winsymlinks:native, while with winsymlinks:nativestrict the symlink(2) system call will immediately fail.

  For more information on symbolic links, see Section 3.1.6.

3.5.2 Obsolete options

Certain CYGWIN options available in past releases have been removed in Cygwin 1.7 for one reason or another. These obsolete options are listed below.

- (no)binmode - This option has been removed because all file opens default to binary mode, unless the open mode has been specified explicitly in the open(2) call.

- check_case - This option has been removed in favor of real case sensitivity and the per-mount option "posix=[0|1]". For more information, read the documentation in Section 3.1.2 and Section 3.4.5.

- codepage:[ansi|oem] - This option controlled which character set is used for file and console operations. Since Cygwin is now doing all character conversion by itself, depending on the application call to the setlocale() function, and in turn by the setting of the environment variables $LANG, $LC_ALL, or $LC_CTYPE, this setting became superfluous.

- (no)envcache - Originally, envcache controlled caching of environment variable conversion between Win32 and POSIX. The default setting works fine, the option was just useless.

- forkchunk:[intval] - This option allowed to influence the fork() function in the way the memory of the parent process gets copied to the child process. This functionality was only useful for Windows 95/98/Me.

- (no)ntea - This option has been removed since it only fakes security which is considered dangerous and useless. It also created an uncontrollably large file on FAT and was entirely useless on FAT32.

- (no)ntsec - This option has been removed in favor of the per-mount option "acl"/"noacl". For more information, read the documentation in Section 3.1.2.

- (no)server - Originally this option had to be enabled on the client side to use features only available when running **cygserver**. This option has been removed because Cygwin now always tries to contact cygserver if a function is called which requires cygserver being available. For more information, read the documentation in Section 3.7.

- (no)smbntsec - This option has been removed in favor of the per-mount option "acl"/"noacl". For more information, read the documentation in Section 3.1.2.

- (no)strip_title - Removed because setting the Window title can be controlled by the application via Escape sequences.

- (no)title - Removed because setting the Window title can be controlled by the application via Escape sequences.

- (no)transparent_exe - This option has been removed because the behaviour it switched on is now the standard behaviour in Cygwin.

- (no)traverse - This option has been removed because traverse checking is not quite correctly implemented by Microsoft and it's behaviour has been getting worse with each new OS version. This complicates its usage so the option has been removed for now.

- (no)tty - If set, Cygwin enabled extra support (i.e., termios) for UNIX-like ttys in the Windows console. This option has been removed because it can be easily replaced by using a terminal like **mintty**, and it does not work well with some Windows programs.

- (no)upcaseenv - This option could be used to convert all environment variables to uppercase. This was the default behavior in releases prior to Cygwin 1.7. Since keeping the case of environment variables intact is POSIXly correct, Cygwin now does not change the case of environment variables, except for a restricted set to maintain minimal backward compatibility. The current list of always uppercased variables is:

```
COMMONPROGRAMFILES
COMSPEC
PATH
SYSTEMDRIVE
SYSTEMROOT
TEMP
TMP
WINDIR
```

3.6 POSIX accounts, permission, and security

This section discusses how the Windows security model is utilized in Cygwin to implement POSIX account information, POSIX-like permissions, and how the Windows authentication model is used to allow cygwin applications to switch users in a POSIX-like fashion.

The setting of POSIX-like file and directory permissions is controlled by the mount option (no)acl which is set to acl by default.

We start with a short overview. Note that this overview must be necessarily short. If you want to learn more about the Windows security model, see the Access Control article in MSDN documentation.

POSIX concepts and in particular the POSIX security model are not discussed here, but assumed to be understood by the reader. If you don't know the POSIX security model, search the web for beginner documentation.

3.6.1 Brief overview of Windows security

In the Windows security model, almost any "object" is securable. "Objects" are files, processes, threads, semaphores, etc.

Every object has a data structure attached, called a "security descriptor" (SD). The SD contains all information necessary to control who can access an object, and to determine what they are allowed to do to or with it. The SD of an object consists of five parts:

- Flags which control several aspects of this SD. This is not discussed here.
- The SID of the object owner.
- The SID of the object owner group.
- A list of "Access Control Entries" (ACE), called the "Discretionary Access Control List" (DACL).
- Another list of ACEs, called the "Security Access Control List" (SACL), which doesn't matter for our purpose. We ignore it here.

Every ACE contains a so-called "Security IDentifier" (SID) and other stuff which is explained a bit later. Let's talk about the SID first.

A SID is a unique identifier for users, groups, computers and Active Directory (AD) domains. SIDs are basically comparable to POSIX user ids (UIDs) and group ids (GIDs), but are more complicated because they are unique across multiple machines or domains. A SID is a structure of multiple numerical values. There's a convenient convention to type SIDs, as a string of numerical fields separated by hyphen characters. Here's an example:

SID of a machine "foo":

```
S-1-5-21-165875785-1005667432-441284377
```

SID of a user "johndoe" of the system "foo":

```
S-1-5-21-165875785-1005667432-441284377-1023
```

The first field is always "S", which is just a notational convention to show that this is a SID. The second field is the version number of the SID structure, So far there exists only one version of SIDs, so this field is always 1. The third and fourth fields represent the "authority" which can be thought of as a type or category of SIDs. There are a couple of builtin accounts and accounts with very special meaning which have certain well known values in these third and fourth fields. However, computer and domain SIDs always start with "S-1-5-21". The next three fields, all 32 bit values, represent the unique 96 bit identifier of the computer system. This is a hopefully unique value all over the world, but in practice it's sufficient if the computer SIDs are unique within a single Windows network.

As you can see in the above example, SIDs of users (and groups) are identical to the computer SID, except for an additional part, the so-called "relative identifier" (RID). So the SID of a user is always uniquely attached to the system on which the account has been generated.

It's a bit different in domains. The domain has its own SID, and that SID is identical to the SID of the first domain controller, on which the domain is created. Domain user SIDs look exactly like the computer user SIDs, the leading part is just the domain SID and the RID is created when the user is created.

Ok, consider you created a new domain "bar" on some new domain controller and you would like to create a domain account "johndoe":

SID of a domain "bar.local":

```
S-1-5-21-186985262-1144665072-740312968
```

SID of a user "johndoe" in the domain "bar.local":

```
S-1-5-21-186985262-1144665072-740312968-1207
```

So you now have two accounts called johndoe, one account created on the machine "foo", one created in the domain "bar.local". Both have different SIDs and not even the RID is the same. How do the systems know it's the same account? After all, the name is the same, right? The answer is, these accounts are **not** identical. All machines on the network will treat these SIDs as identifying two separate accounts. One is "FOO\johndoe", the other one is "BAR\johndoe" or "johndoe@bar.local". Different SID, different account. Full stop.

Starting with Cygwin 1.7.34, Cygwin uses an automatic, internal translation from Windows SID to POSIX UID/GID. This mechanism, which is the preferred method for the SID<=>UID/GID mapping, is described in detail in Section 3.6.2.

Prior to Cygwin 1.7.34, the last part of the SID, the so called "Relative IDentifier" (RID), was by default used as UID and/or GID when you created the /etc/passwd and /etc/group files using the **mkpasswd** and **mkgroup** tools. These tools as well as reading accounts from /etc/passwd and /etc/group files is still present in recent versions of Cygwin, but you should switch to the aforementioned automatic translation, unless you have very specific needs. Again, see Section 3.6.2 for the details.

Do you still remember the SIDs with special meaning? In offical notation they are called "well-known SIDs". For example, POSIX has no GID for the group of "all users" or "world" or "others". The last three rwx bits in a unix-style permission value just represent the permissions for "everyone who is not the owner or is member of the owning group". Windows has a SID for these poor souls, the "Everyone" SID. Other well-known SIDs represent circumstances under which a process is running, rather than actual users or groups. Here are a few examples for well-known SIDs:

```
Everyone                        S-1-1-0     Simply everyone...
Batch                           S-1-5-3     Processes started via the task
            scheduler are member of this group.
Interactive     S-1-5-4     Only processes of users which are
            logged in via an interactive
            session are members here.
Authenticated Users             S-1-5-11    Users which have gone through
                                            the authentication process and
            survived.  Anonymously accessing
            users are not incuded here.
SYSTEM                          S-1-5-18    A special account which has all
            kinds of dangerous rights, sort of
            an uber-root account.
```

For a full list please refer to the MSDN document Well-known SIDs. The Cygwin package called "csih" provides a tool, /usr/lib/csih/getAccountName.exe, which can be used to print the (possibly localized) name for the various well-known SIDS.

Naturally, well-known SIDs are the same on each machine, so they are not unique to a machine or domain. They have the same meaning across the Windows network.

Additionally, there are a couple of well-known builtin groups, which have the same SID on every machine and which have certain user rights by default:

```
administrators                  S-1-5-32-544
users                           S-1-5-32-545
guests                          S-1-5-32-546
...
```

For instance, every account is usually member in the "Users" group. All administrator accounts are member of the "Administrators" group. That's all about it as far as single machines are involved. In a domain environment it's a bit more tricky. Since these SIDs are not unique to a machine, every domain user and every domain group can be a member of these well known groups. Consider the domain group "Domain Admins". This group is by default in the "Administrators" group. Let's assume the above computer called "foo" is a member machine of the domain "bar.local". If you stick the user "BAR\johndoe" into the group "Domain Admins", this guy will automatically be a member of the administrators group on "foo" when logging on to "foo". Neat, isn't it?

Back to ACE and ACL. POSIX is able to create three different permissions, the permissions for the owner, for the group and for the world. In contrast the Windows ACL has a potentially infinite number of members... as long as they fit into 64K. Every member is an ACE. ACE consist of three parts:

- The type of the ACE (allow ACE or deny ACE).
- Permission bits, 32 of them.
- The SID for which the permissions are allowed or denied.

The two (for us) important types of ACEs are the "access allowed ACE" and the "access denied ACE". As the names imply, the allow ACE tells the system to allow the given permissions to the SID, the deny ACE results in denying the specific permission bits.

The possible permissions on objects are more detailed than in POSIX. For example, the permission to delete an object is different from the permission to change object data, and even changing object data can be separated into different permission bits for different kind of data. But there's a problem with the definition of a "correct" ACL which disallows mapping of certain POSIX permissions cleanly. See Section 3.6.3.

POSIX is able to create only three different permissions? Not quite. Newer operating systems and file systems on POSIX systems also provide access control lists. Two different APIs exist for accessing these ACLs, the Solaris API and the POSIX API. Cygwin implements the original Solaris API to access Windows ACLs in a Unixy way. Online man pages for the Solaris ACL API can be found on http://docs.oracle.com. For an overview see acl(5).

3.6.2 Mapping Windows accounts to POSIX accounts

For as long as Cygwin has existed, it has stored user and group information in /etc/passwd and /etc/group files. Under the assumption that these files would never be too large, the first process in a process tree, as well as every execing process within the tree would parse them into structures in memory. Thus every Cygwin process would contain an expanded copy of the full information from /etc/passwd and /etc/group.

This approach has a few downsides. One of them is that the idea that these files will always be small, is flawed. Another one is that reading the entire file is most of the time entirely useless, since most processes only need information on their own user and the primary group. Last but not least, the passwd and group files have to be maintained separately from the already existing Windows user databases, the local SAM and Active Directory.

On the other hand, we have to have this mapping between Windows SIDs and POSIX uid/gid values, so we need a mechanism to convert SIDs to uid/gid values and vice versa.

Microsoft "Services for UNIX" (SFU) (deprecated since Windows 8/Server 2012) never used passwd/group files. Rather, SFU used a fixed, computational mapping between SIDs and POSIX uid/gid which even has Active Directory support. It allows us to generate uid/gid values from SIDs and vice versa. The mechanism is documented, albeit in a confusing way and spread over multiple MSDN articles.

Starting with Cygwin 1.7.34, Cygwin utilizes an approach inspired by the mapping method as implemented by SFU, with a few differences for backward compatibility and to handle some border cases differently.

3.6.2.1 Mapping Windows SIDs to POSIX uid/gid values

The following description assumes you're comfortable with the concept of Windows SIDs and RIDs. For a brief introduction, see Section 3.6.1.

Cygwin's mapping between SIDs and uid/gid values works in two ways.

- Read /etc/passwd and/etc/group files if they exist, just as in the olden days, mainly for backward compatibility.
- If no files are present, or if an entry is missing in the files, ask Windows.

At least, that's the default behaviour now. It will be configurable using a file /etc/nsswitch.conf, which is discussed in Section 3.6.2.4. Let's explore the default for now.

If the passwd or group files are present, they will be scanned on demand as soon as a mapping from SIDs to uid/gid or account names is required. The new mechanism will never read the entire file into memory, but only scan for the requested entry and cache this one in memory.

If no entry is found, or no passwd or group file was present, Cygwin will ask the OS.

Note

If the first process in a Cygwin process tree determines that no /etc/passwd or /etc/group file is present, no other process in the entire process tree will try to read the files later on. This is done for self-preservation. It's rather bad if the uid or gid of a user changes during the lifetime of a process tree.

For the same reason, if you delete the /etc/passwd or /etc/group file, this will be ignored. The passwd and group records read from the files will persist in memory until either a new /etc/passwd or /etc/group is created, or you exit all processes in the current process tree.

See the note in Section 3.6.2.4 for some comprehensive examples.

So if we've drawn a blank reading the files, we're going to ask the OS. First thing, we ask the local machine for the SID or the username. The OS functions LookupAccountSid and LookupAccountName are pretty intelligent. They have all the stuff built in to ask for any account of the local machine, the Active Directory domain of the machine, the Global Catalog of the forest of the domain, as well as any trusted domain of our forest for the information. One OS call and we're practically done...

Except, the calls only return the mapping between SID, account name and the account's domain. We don't have a mapping to POSIX uid/gid and we're missing information on the user's home dir and login shell.

Let's discuss the SID<=>uid/gid mapping first. Here's how it works.

- Well-known SIDs in the NT_AUTHORITY domain of the S-1-5-RID type, or aliases of the S-1-5-32-RID type are mapped to the uid/gid value RID. Examples:

```
"SYSTEM"  S-1-5-18                    <=> uid/gid: 18
"Users"   S-1-5-32-545               <=> uid/gid: 545
```

- Other well-known SIDs in the NT_AUTHORITY domain (S-1-5-X-RID):

```
S-1-5-X-RID                           <=> uid/gid: 0x1000 * X + RID
```

Example:

```
    "NTLM Authentication" S-1-5-64-10      <=> uid/gid: 0x4000A == 262154
```

- Other well-known SIDs:

```
    S-1-X-Y                                <=> uid/gid: 0x10000 + 0x100 * X + Y
```

  Example:

```
    "LOCAL" S-1-2-0                        <=> uid/gid: 0x10200 == 66048
    "Creator Group" S-1-3-1                <=> uid/gid: 0x10301 == 66305
```

- Logon SIDs: The LogonSid of the current user's session is converted to the fixed uid 0xfff == 4095 and named "CurrentSession". Any other LogonSid is converted to the fixed uid 0xffe == 4094 and named "OtherSession".

- Mandatory Labels:

```
    S-1-16-RID                             <=> uid/gid: 0x60000 + RID
```

  Example:

```
    "Medium Mandatory Level" S-1-16-8192 <=> uid/gid: 0x62000 == 401408
```

- Accounts from the local machine's user DB (SAM):

```
    S-1-5-21-X-Y-Z-RID                     <=> uid/gid: 0x30000 + RID
```

  Example:

```
    "Administrator" S-1-5-21-X-Y-Z-500     <=> uid/gid: 0x301f4 == 197108
```

- Accounts from the machine's primary domain:

```
    S-1-5-21-X-Y-Z-RID                     <=> uid/gid: 0x100000 + RID
```

  Example:

```
    "Domain Users" S-1-5-21-X-Y-Z-513      <=> uid/gid: 0x100201 == 1049089
```

- Accounts from a trusted domain of the machine's primary domain:

```
    S-1-5-21-X-Y-Z-RID                     <=> uid/gid: trustPosixOffset(domain) + RID
```

`trustPosixOffset`? This needs a bit of explanation. This value exists in Windows domains already since before Active Directory days. What happens is this. If you create a domain trust between two domains, a trustedDomain entry will be added to both databases. It describes how *this* domain trusts the *other* domain. One attribute of a trust is a 32 bit value called `trustPosixOffset` For each new trust, `trustPosixOffset` will get some automatic value. In recent AD domain implementations, the first trusted domain will get `trustPosixOffset` set to 0x80000000. Following domains will get lower values. Unfortunately the domain admins are allowed to set the `trustPosixOffset` value for each trusted domain to some arbitrary 32 bit value, no matter what the other `trustPosixOffset` are set to, thus allowing any kind of collisions between the `trustPosixOffset` values of domains. That's not exactly helpful, but as the user of this value, we have to *trust* the domain admins to set `trustPosixOffset` to sensible values, or to keep it at the system chosen defaults.

So, for the first (or only) trusted domain of your domain, the automatic offset is 0x80000000. An example for a user of that trusted domain is

```
    S-1-5-21-X-Y-Z-1234                    <=> uid/gid 0x800004d2 == 2147484882
```

There's one problem with this approach. Assuming you're running in the context of a local SAM user on a domain member machine. Local users don't have the right to fetch this kind of domain information from the DC, they'll get permission denied. In this case Cygwin will fake a sensible `trustPosixOffset` value.

Another problem is if the AD administrators chose an unreasonably small `trustPosixOffset` value. Anything below the hexadecimal value 0x100000 (the POSIX offset of the primary domain) is bound to produce collisions with system accounts as well as local accounts. The right thing to do in this case is to notify your administrator of the problem and to ask for moving the offset to a more reasonable value. However, to reduce the probability for collisions, Cygwin overrides this offset with a sensible fixed replacement offset.

- Local accounts from another machine in the network:

  There's no SID<=>uid/gid mapping implemented for this case. The problem is, there's no way to generate a bijective mapping. There's no central place which keeps an analogue of the `trustPosixOffset`, and there's the additional problem that the LookupAccountSid and LookupAccountName functions cannnot resolve the SIDs, unless they know the name of the machine this SID comes from. And even then it will probably suffer a `Permission denied` error when trying to ask the machine for its local account.

Now we have a semi-bijective mapping between SIDs and POSIX uid/gid values, but given that we have potentially users and groups in different domains having the same name, how do we uniquely distinguish between them by name? Well, we can do that by making their names unique in a per-machine way. Dependent on the domain membership of the account, and dependent of the machine being a domain member or not, the user and group names will be generated using a domain prefix and a separator character between domain and account name. The separator character is the plus sign, +.

- Well-known and builtin accounts will be named as in Windows:

  ```
  "SYSTEM", "LOCAL", "Medium Mandatory Level", ...
  ```

- If the machine is not a domain member machine, only local accounts can be resolved into names, so for ease of use, just the account names are used as Cygwin user/group names:

  ```
  "corinna", "bigfoot", "None", ...
  ```

- If the machine is a domain member machine, all accounts from the primary domain of the machine are mapped to Cygwin names without domain prefix:

  ```
  "corinna", "bigfoot", "Domain Users", ...
  ```

  while accounts from other domains are prepended by their domain:

  ```
  "DOMAIN1+corinna", "DOMAIN2+bigfoot", "DOMAIN3+Domain Users", ...
  ```

- Local machine accounts of a domain member machine get a Cygwin user name the same way as accounts from another domain: The local machine name gets prepended:

  ```
  "MYMACHINE+corinna", "MYMACHINE+bigfoot", "MYMACHINE+None", ...
  ```

- If LookupAccountSid fails, Cygwin checks the accounts against the known trusted domains. If the account is from one of the trusted domains, an artificial account name is created. It consists of the domain name, and a special name created from the account RID:

  ```
  "MY_DOM+User(1234)", "MY_DOM+Group(5678)"
  ```

Otherwise we know nothing about this SID, so it will be mapped to the fake accounts `Unknown+User`/`Unknown+Group` with uid/gid -1.

3.6.2.2 Caching account information

The information fetched from the Windows account database or the `/etc/passwd` and `/etc/group` files is cached by the process. The cached information is inherited by Cygwin child processes. A Cygwin process invoked from a Windows command, such as CMD.exe, will start a new Cygwin process tree and the caching starts from scratch (unless **cygserver** is running, but read on).

While usually working fine, this has some drawbacks. Consider a shell calling **id**. **id** fetches all group information from the current token and caches them. Unfortunately **id** doesn't start any child processes, so the information is lost as soon as **id** exits.

But there's another caching mechanism available. If **cygserver** is running it will provide passwd and group entry caching for all processes in every Cygwin process tree started after **cygserver**. So, if you start a Cygwin Terminal and **cygserver** is running at the time, **mintty**, the shell, and all child processes will use **cygserver** caching. If you start a Cygwin Terminal and **cygserver** is not running at the time, none of the processes started inside this terminal window will use **cygserver** caching.

The advantage of **cygserver** caching is that it's system-wide and, as long as **cygserver** is running, unforgetful. Every Cygwin process on the system will have the **cygserver** cache at its service. Additionally, all information requested from **cygserver** once, will be cached inside the process itself and, again, propagated to child processes.

If you automatically start Cygwin processes as Windows services at system startup, you may wish to consider starting **cygserver** first in order to take advantage of this system-wide caching. To assure that **cygserver** has started prior to starting **sshd** or other Cygwin processes, you may wish to create service startup dependencies. **Cygserver** should probably wait for Windows TCPIP and AFD services before it starts, and then other Cygwin process should start after **cygserver**. Example Windows commands to accomplish this (after the services already exist) are shown below. You will need an administrative prompt to run the **sc config** commands.

```
# Delay Cygserver until TCPIP and AFD have started
# Note the (odd) required space character after "depend="

sc config cygserver depend= tcpip/afd

# Delay sshd until after Cygserver has started
# Again note the (odd) required space character after "depend="

sc config sshd depend= cygserver

# View the Cygserver service details

sc qc cygserver
```

Note that this **sc config** command *replaces* any existing dependencies. The above changes will not impact the running instance, only future instances.

```
# To remove all dependencies from the cygserver service

sc config cygserver depend= /
```

3.6.2.3 Cygwin user names, home dirs, login shells

Obviously, if you don't maintain `passwd` and `group` files, you need to have a way to maintain the other fields of a passwd entry as well. A couple of things come to mind:

- You want to use a Cygwin username different from your Windows username.

Note

This is only supported via `/etc/passwd`. A Cygwin username maintained in the Windows user databases would require very costly (read: slow) search operations.

- You want to change the primary group of a user. For AD accounts this is not supported. The primary group of a user is always the Windows primary group set in Active Directory and can't be changed. For SAM accounts, you can add the primary group to the SAM `description` field of the user. See Section 3.6.2.4.10 for more info.
- You want a home dir different from the default `/home/$USERNAME`.
- You want to specify a different login shell than `/bin/bash`.
- You want to add specific content to the pw_gecos field.

For simple needs you can create `/etc/passwd` and/or `/etc/group` files with entries for your account and tweak that.

For bigger installations, maintaining per-client files is rather troublesome. Also, no two environments are the same, so the needs are pretty different. Therefore Cygwin supports configuring how to fetch home directory, login shell, and gecos information in /etc/nsswitch.conf. See the next section for detailed information how to configure Cygwin's account handling.

3.6.2.4 The /etc/nsswitch.conf file

On Linux and some other UNIXy OSes, we have a file called /etc/nsswitch.conf. Among other things, it determines how passwd and group entries are generated. That's what Cygwin now provides as well.

The /etc/nsswitch.conf file is optional. If you don't have one, Cygwin uses sensible defaults.

Note

The /etc/nsswitch.conf file is read exactly once by the first process of a Cygwin process tree. If there was no /etc/nsswitch.conf file when this first process started, then no other process in the running Cygwin process tree will try to read the file.

If you create or change /etc/nsswitch.conf, you have to restart all Cygwin processes that need to see the change. If the process you want to see the change is a child of another process, you need to restart all of that process's parents, too.

For example, if you run **vim** inside the default Cygwin Terminal, **vim** is a child of your shell, which is a child of **mintty**. If you edit /etc/nsswitch.conf in that **vim** instance, your shell won't immediately see the change, nor will **vim** if you restart it from that same shell instance. This is because both are getting their nsswitch information from their ancestor, **mintty**. You have to start a fresh terminal window for the change to take effect.

By contrast, if you leave that Cygwin Terminal window open after making the change to /etc/nsswitch.conf, then restart a Cygwin service like **cron**, **cron** will see the change, because it is not a child of **mintty** or any other Cygwin process. (Technically, it is a child of **cygrunsrv**, but that instance also restarts when you restart the service.)

The reason we point all this out is that the requirements for restarting things are not quite as stringent as when you replace cygwin1.dll. If you have three process trees, you have three independent copies of the nsswitch information. If you start a fresh process tree, it will see the changes. As long as any process in an existing process tree remains running, all processes in that tree will continue to use the old information.

So, what settings can we perform with /etc/nsswitch.conf? Let's start with an example /etc/nsswitch.conf file set up to all default values:

```
# /etc/nsswitch.conf
passwd: files db
group:  files db

db_enum:   cache builtin
db_home:   /home/%U
db_shell:  /bin/bash
db_gecos:  <empty>
```

3.6.2.4.1 The /etc/nsswitch.conf syntax

The first line, starting with a hash # is a comment. The hash character starts a comment, just as in shell scripts. Everything up to the end of the line is ignored. So this:

```
foo:  bar # baz
```

means, set "foo" to value "bar", ignore everything after the hash.

The other lines define the available settings. The first word up to a colon is a keyword. Note that the colon *must* follow immediately after the keyword. This is a valid line:

```
foo: bar
```

This is not valid:

```
foo : bar
```

Apart from this restriction, the reminder of the line can have as many spaces and TABs as you like.

3.6.2.4.2 The `passwd:` and `group:` settings

The two lines starting with the keywords `passwd:` and `group:` define where Cygwin gets its passwd and group information from. `files` means, fetch the information from the corresponding file in the /etc directory. `db` means, fetch the information from the Windows account databases, the SAM for local accounts, Active Directory for domain account. Examples:

```
passwd: files
```

Read passwd entries only from /etc/passwd.

```
group: db
```

Read group entries only from SAM/AD.

```
group: files # db
```

Read group entries only from `/etc/group` (db is only a comment).

```
passwd: files db
```

Read passwd entries from `/etc/passwd`. If a user account isn't found, try to find it in SAM or AD. This is the default for both, passwd and group information.

```
group: db files
```

This is a valid entry, but the order will be ignored by Cygwin. If both settings, `files` and `db` are specified, Cygwin will always try the files first, then the db.

`passwd:` and `group:` are the two basic settings defining where to get the account information from. The following settings starting with `db_` define certain aspects of the Windows account database search and how to generate `passwd` and `group` information from the database.

3.6.2.4.3 The `db_enum:` setting

`db_enum:` defines the depth of a database search, if an application calls one of the enumeration functions getpwent or getgrent. The problem with these functions is, they neither allow to define how many entries will be enumerated when calling them in a loop, nor do they allow to add some filter criteria. They were designed back in the days, when only `/etc/passwd` and `/etc/group` files existed and the number of user accounts on a typical UNIX system was seldomly a three-digit number.

These days, with user and group databases sometimes going in the six-digit range, they are a potential burden. For that reason, Cygwin does not enumerate all user or group accounts by default, but rather just a very small list, consisting only of the accounts cached in memory by the current process, as well as a handful of predefined builtin accounts.

`db_enum:` allows to specify the accounts to enumerate in a fine-grained manner. It takes a list of sources as argument:

```
db_enum:  source1 source2 ...
```

The recognized sources are the following:

none No output from getpwent/getgrent at all.

all The opposite. Enumerates accounts from all known sources, including all trusted domains.

cache Enumerate all accounts currently cached in memory.

builtin Enumerate the predefined builtin accounts for backward compatibility. These are five passwd accounts (SYSTEM, LocalService, NetworkService, Administrators, TrustedInstaller) and two group accounts (SYSTEM and TrustedInstaller).

files Enumerate the accounts from `/etc/passwd` or `/etc/group`.

local Enumerate all accounts from the local SAM.

primary Enumerate all accounts from the primary domain.

alltrusted Enumerate all accounts from all trusted domains.

some.domain Enumerate all accounts from the trusted domain some.domain. The trusted domain can be given as Netbios flat name (MY_DOMAIN) or as dns domain name (my_domain.corp). In contrast to the aforementioned fixed source keywords, distinct domain names are caseinsensitive. Only domains which are actually trusted domains are enumerated. Unknown domains are simply ignored.

Please note that `getpwent`/`getgrent` do *not* test if an account was already listed from another source, so an account can easily show up twice or three times. Such a test would be rather tricky, nor does the Linux implementation perform such test. Here are a few examples for `/etc/nsswitch.conf`:

```
db_enum: none
```

No output from `getpwent`/`getgrent` at all. The first call to the function immediately returns a NULL pointer.

```
db_enum: cache files
```

Enumerate all accounts cached by the current process, plus all entries from either the /etc/passwd or /etc/group file.

```
db_enum: cache local primary
```

Enumerate all accounts cached by the current process, all accounts from the SAM of the local machine, and all accounts from the primary domain of the machine.

```
db_enum: local primary alltrusted
```

Enumerate the accounts from the machine's SAM, from the primary domain of the machine, and from all trusted domains.

```
db_enum: primary domain1.corp sub.domain.corp domain2.net
```

Enumerate the accounts from the primary domain and from the domains domain1.corp, sub.domain.corp and domain2.net.

```
db_enum: all
```

Enumerate everything and the kitchen sink.

3.6.2.4.4 Settings defining how to create the `passwd` entry

`/etc/nsswitch.conf` supports three settings to configure where to get the pw_dir, pw_shell, and pw_gecos content of a `passwd` entry from:

```
db_home:  schema...     # Define how to fetch the pw_dir entry.
db_shell: schema...     # Define how to fetch the pw_shell entry.
db_gecos: schema...     # Define how to fetch the pw_gecos entry.
```

"schema..." is a list of up to four space-separated schemata:

```
db_FOO: schema1 schema2 ...
```

When generating a passwd entry, Cygwin tries the schemata in order. If the first schema returns an empty string, it skips to the second, and so on. Schemata only supported on AD are silently skipped for SAM accounts and on non-AD machines.

Four schemata are predefined, two schemata are variable. The predefined schemata are the following:

windows Utilizes typical Windows settings. Supported for AD and SAM accounts.

cygwin Utilizes the cygwinUser AD schema extension. This schema extension is available via a schema extension file `/usr/share/cygwin/cygwin.ldif`. See Section 3.6.2.4.8 for more information.

unix Utilizes the posixAccount schema attributes per RFC 2307. The posixAccount schema is available by default since Windows Server 2003 R2, but typically only utilized when installing the Active Directory "Server for NIS" feature (which is deprecated since Server 2012 R2). See also Section 3.6.2.4.9.

desc Utilizes XML-style attributes in the description attribute. Supported for AD and SAM accounts. See Section 3.6.2.4.10 for a more detailed description.

The variable schemata are as follows. Note that the leading characters (@ and /) are an integral part of the definition.

@ad_attribute `ad_attribute` is any arbitrary AD attribute name which should (ideally) be available in the User class or in any attached auxiliary class. It's always treated as a single string argument. Only the first string of a multi-string attributes will be read.

/path An arbitrary string, typically a path. The leading slash is required. Given that a single, fixed path for all users only makes marginal sense, the /path schema supports wildcards. A wildcard is a per-cent (%) character, followed by another character giving the meaning. The supported wildcard characters are:

%u The Cygwin username (that's lowercase u).

%U The Windows username (that's uppercase U).

%D Windows domain in NetBIOS style.

%H Windows home directory in POSIX style. Note that, for the `db_home:` setting, this only makes sense right after the preceeding slash, as in

```
db_home:  /%H/cygwin
```

%_ Since space and TAB characters are used to separate the schemata, a space in the filename has to be given as %_ (that's an underscore).

%% A per-cent character.

Any other %X expression is treated as if the character X has been given alone.

The exact meaning of a schema depends on the setting it's used for. The following sections explain the settings in detail.

3.6.2.4.5 The db_home: setting

The `db_home:` setting defines how Cygwin fetches the user's home directory, or, more precise, the content of the `pw_dir` member of the user's passwd entry. The following list describes the meaning of each schema when used with `db_home:`

windows The user's home directory is set to the same directory which is used as Windows home directory. This is the home Directory AD attribute. For SAM accounts, this is equivalent to the "Home folder" setting in SAM. If both attributes are unset, Cygwin falls back to the user's local profile directory, typically something along the lines of `C:\Users\ $USERNAME`. Of course, the Windows directory is converted to POSIX-style by Cygwin.

cygwin AD only: The user's home directory is set to the POSIX path given in the `cygwinHome` attribute from the `cygwinUser` auxiliary class. See also Section 3.6.2.4.8.

unix AD only: The user's home directory is set to the POSIX path given in the `unixHomeDirectory` attribute from the `posixAccount` auxiliary class. See also Section 3.6.2.4.9.

desc The user's home directory is set to the POSIX path given in the home="..." XML-alike setting in the user's `description` attribute in SAM or AD. See Section 3.6.2.4.10 for a detailed description.

@ad_attribute AD only: The user's home directory is set to the path given in the `ad_attribute` attribute. The path can be given as Windows or POSIX path.

/path The user's home directory is set to the given POSIX path. Remember the wildcards described in Section 3.6.2.4.4.

Fallback If none of the schemes given for `db_home:` define a non-empty directory, the user's home directory is set to `/home/ $USERNAME`.

As has been briefly mentioned before, the default setting for db_home: is

```
db_home: /home/%U
```

So by default, Cygwin just sets the home dir to /home/$USERNAME.

3.6.2.4.6 The db_shell: setting

The db_shell: setting defines how Cygwin fetches the user's login shell, the content of the pw_shell member of the user's passwd entry. The following list describes the meaning of each schema when used with db_shell:

windows The windows schema is ignored for now. The logical choice would be CMD, but that introduces some problems, for instance the fact that CMD has no concept of running as login shell. This may change in future.

cygwin AD only: The user's home directory is set to the POSIX path given in the cygwinShell attribute from the cygwin User auxiliary class. See also Section 3.6.2.4.8.

unix AD only: The user's login shell is set to the POSIX path given in the loginShell attribute from the posixAccount auxiliary class. See also Section 3.6.2.4.9.

desc The user's login shell is set to the POSIX path given in the shell="..." XML-alike setting in the user's description attribute in SAM or AD. See Section 3.6.2.4.10 for a detailed description.

@ad_attribute AD only: The user's login shell is set to the path given in the ad_attribute attribute. The path can be given as Windows or POSIX path.

/path The user's login shell is set to the given POSIX path. Albeit not being as important here, the wildcards described in Section 3.6.2.4.4 are also available for specifying a login shell path.

Fallback If none of the schemes given for db_shell: define a non-empty pathname, the user's login shell is set to /bin/bash.

As for db_home:, the default setting for db_shell: is pretty much a constant

```
db_shell: /bin/bash
```

3.6.2.4.7 The db_gecos: setting

The db_gecos: setting defines how to fetch additional content for the pw_gecos member of the user's passwd entry. There's always a fixed, Cygwin-specific part in the pw_gecos field for identifying the account. However, an administrator might want to add informative content like, for instance, the user's full name. That's what the db_gecos: setting is for. The following list describes the meaning of each schema when used with db_gecos:

windows Add the AD displayName attribute or, for SAM accounts, the "Full name" entry to the pw_gecos field.

cygwin AD only: The content of the cygwinGecos attribute from the cygwinUser auxiliary class is added to pw_gecos. See also Section 3.6.2.4.8.

unix AD only: The content of the gecos attribute from the posixAccount auxiliary class is added to pw_gecos. See also Section 3.6.2.4.9.

desc The content of the gecos="..." XML-alike setting in the user's description attribute in SAM or AD is added to pw_gecos. See Section 3.6.2.4.10 for a detailed description.

@ad_attribute AD only: The content of the ad_attribute attribute is added to pw_gecos.

/path The string following the slash is added to pw_gecos. Here, the wildcards described in Section 3.6.2.4.4 may come in handy.

Fallback If none of the schemes given for db_gecos: define a non-empty pathname, nothing is added to pw_gecos.

The default setting for db_gecos: is the empty string.

3.6.2.4.8 The `cygwin` schema

The `cygwin` schema is based on a Cygwin-specific Active Directory schema extension. Using this schema extension allows to maintain Cygwin-specific settings entirely within AD, without colliding with any other schema.

The cygwin schema extension is available in a default Cygwin installation in the file `/usr/share/cygwin/cygwin.ldif`. To install the schema extension, you have to be schema admin, and you have to run the **ldifde** command on the schema master. The installation itself is rather simple. Assuming you're schema admin and running a shell with administrative privileges:

```
$ cd /usr/share/cygwin
$ ldifde -i -f cygwin.ldif -k -c "CN=schema,CN=Configuration,DC=X" #schemaNamingContext
```

Afterwards, the auxiliary class `cygwinUser` is attached to the class `User`, and the auxiliary class `cygwinGroup` is attached to the class `Group`. The new attributes can be immediately edited using **ADSI Edit**.

At the time of writing the following attributes are utilized by Cygwin:

: `cygwinHome`, : Used as Cygwin home directory with `db_home:cygwin`. See Section 3.6.2.4.5.
: `cygwinShell`, : Used as Cygwin login shell with `db_shell:cygwin`. See Section 3.6.2.4.6.
: `cygwinGecos`, : Content will be added to the pw_gecos field with `db_gecos:cygwin`. See Section 3.6.2.4.7.

3.6.2.4.9 The `unix` schema

The `unix` schema utilizes the `posixAccount` attribute extension. This is one of two schema extensions which are connected to AD accounts, available by default starting with Windows Server 2003 R2. They are usually **not set**, unless used by the Active Directory `Server for NIS` feature (deprecated since Server 2012 R2). Two schemata are interesting for Cygwin, `posixAccount`, connected to user accounts, and `posixGroup`, connected to group accounts. Both follow the description of RFC 2307, an Approach for Using LDAP as a Network Information Service. The user attributes utilized by Cygwin are:

: `unixHomeDirectory`, : Used as Cygwin home directory with `db_home:unix`. See Section 3.6.2.4.5.
: `loginShell`, : Used as Cygwin login shell with `db_shell:unix`. See Section 3.6.2.4.6.
: `gecos`, : Content will be added to the pw_gecos field with `db_gecos:unix`. See Section 3.6.2.4.7.
: `uidNumber`, : See Section 3.6.2.5 and Section 3.6.2.6.

The group attributes utilized by Cygwin are:

: `gidNumber`, : See Section 3.6.2.5 and Section 3.6.2.6.

Apart from power shell scripting or inventing new CLI tools, these attributes can be changed using the `Attribute Editor` tab in the user properties dialog of the `Active Directory Users and Computers` MMC snap-in. Alternatively, if the `Server for NIS` administration feature has been installed, there will be a `UNIX Attributes` tab which contains the required fields, except for the gecos field. Last resort is **ADSI Edit**.

3.6.2.4.10 The `desc` schema

When using user accounts from the local account database, the SAM, there are only a very limited number of settings available. In contrast to Active Directory there's no way to add fields to a user's entry. You have to make do with the fields available. The method to utilize the `description` field has been mainly introduced for those accounts, usually the only ones a home user has. However, for symmetry, and because there may be a reason to use this in an AD environment, this schema is also supported for AD users.

Note
The presentation of local user account settings on Windows is confusing, to say the least. The `description` field is not visible at all in the user settings available via the `User Accounts` control settings. And while it's called `Description` in the `Local Users and Groups` MMC snap-in (available, for instance, via the `Computer Management` GUI), in the command line tool **net user** the same field is called `comment`. The latter is especially confusing for AD admins, because the `comment` attribute in AD is called `usercomment` on the command line. Confused? Never mind, you're not the only one...

Fortunately you can utilize the `description` field even if you're running a "home edition" of Windows, by using the command line. The **net user** command allows to set all values in the SAM, even if the GUI is crippled.

A Cygwin SAM comment entry looks like this:

```
<cygwin key="value" key="value" [...] />
```

The supported keys are:

`home="value"`, Sets the Cygwin home dir to value.
`shell="value"`, Sets the Cygwin login shell to value.
`gecos="value"`, Adds the string value to the user's gecos field.

The next two settings are only supported for SAM accounts.

`group="value"`, Sets the Cygwin primary group of the account to value, provided that the user *is* already a member of that group. This allows to override the default `None` primary group for local accounts. One nice idea here is, for instance, group="Users".
`unix="value"`, Sets the NFS/Samba uid of the user to the decimal value. See Section 3.6.2.5 and Section 3.6.2.6.

The <cygwin .../> string can start at any point in the comment, but you have to follow the rules:

- It starts with "<cygwin " and ends with "/>".
- The "cygwin" string and the key names have to be lowercase.
- No spaces between key and "value", just the equal sign.
- The value must be placed within double quotes and it must not contain a double quote itself. The double quotes are required for the decimal values as well!

Note

There's also a length restriction imposed by Windows. The `description` entry has a maximum length of 1023 characters.

CMD example:

```
net user corinna /comment:"<cygwin home=\"/home/foo\"/>"
```

Bash example (use single quotes):

```
net user corinna /comment:'<cygwin home="/home/foo"/>'
```

For changing group comments, use the `net localgroup` command. The supported key/value pair for SAM groups are:

`unix="value"`, Sets the NFS/Samba gid of the group to the decimal value. See Section 3.6.2.5 and Section 3.6.2.6.

3.6.2.5 NFS account mapping

Microsoft's NFS client does not map the uid/gid values on the NFS shares to SIDs. There's no such thing as a (fake) security descriptor returned to the application. Rather, via an undocumented API an application can fetch RFC 1813 compatible NFSv3 stat information from the share. This is what Cygwin is using to show stat information for files on NFS shares.

The problem is, while all other information in this stat record, like timestamps, file size etc., can be used by Cygwin, Cygwin had no way to map the values of the st_uid and st_gid members to a Windows SID for a long time. So it just faked the file owner info and claimed that it's you.

However, SFU has, over time, developed multiple methods to map UNIX uid/gid values on NFS shares to Windows SIDs. You'll find the full documentation of the mapping methods in NFS Identity Mapping in Windows Server 2012

Cygwin now utilizes the RFC 2307 mapping for this purpose. This is most of the time provided by an AD domain, but it could also be a standalone LDAP mapping server. Per RFC 2307, the uid is in the attribute `uidNumber`. For groups, the gid is in the `gidNumber` attribute. See Section 3.6.2.4.9.

When Cygwin stat()s files on an NFS share, it asks the mapping server via LDAP in two different ways, depending on the role of the mapping server.

- If the server is an AD domain controller, it asks for an account with `uidNumber` attribute == `st_uid` field of the stat record returned by NFS. If an account matches, AD returns the Windows SID, so we have an immediate mapping from UNIX uid to a Windows SID, if the user account has a valid `uidNumber` attribute. For groups, the method is the same, just that Cygwin asks for a group with `gidNumber` attribute == `st_gid` field of the stat record.

- If the server is a standalone LDAP mapping server Cygwin asks for the same `uidNumber`/`gidNumber` attributes, but it can't expect that the LDAP server knows anything about Windows SIDs. Rather, the mapping server returns the account name. Cygwin then asks the DC for an account with this name, and if that succeeds, we have a mapping between UNIX uid/gid and Windows SIDs.

The mapping will be cached for the lifetime of the process, and inherited by child processes.

3.6.2.6 Samba account mapping

A fully set up Samba file server with domain integration is running winbindd to map Windows SIDs to artificially created UNIX uids and gids, and this mapping is transparent within the domain, so Cygwin doesn't have to do anything special.

However, setting up winbindd isn't for everybody, and it fails to map Windows accounts to already existing UNIX users or groups. In contrast to NFS, Samba returns security descriptors, but unmapped UNIX accounts get special SIDs:

- A UNIX user account with uid X is mapped to the Windows SID S-1-22-1-X.
- A UNIX group account with gid X is mapped to SID S-1-22-2-X.

As you can see, even though we have SIDs, they just reflect the actual uid/gid values on the UNIX box in the RID value. It's only marginally different from the NFS method, so why not just use the same method as for NFS?

That's what Cygwin will do. If it encounters a S-1-22-x-y SID, it will perform the same RFC 2307 mapping as for NFS shares.

For home users without any Windows domain or LDAP server per RFC 2307, but with a Linux machine running Samba, just add this information to your SAM account. Assuming the uid of your Linux user account is 505 and the gid of your primary group is, say, 100, just add the values to your SAM user and group accounts. The following example assumes you didn't already add something else to the comment field.

To your user's SAM comment (remember: called `Description` in the GUI), add:

```
<cygwin group="Users" unix="505"/>
```

To the `Users` group SAM comment add:

```
<cygwin unix="100"/>
```

This should be sufficient to work on your Samba share and to see all files owned by your Linux user account as your files.

3.6.3 File permissions

On NTFS and if the `noacl` mount option is not specified for a mount point, Cygwin sets file permissions as on POSIX systems. Basically this is done by defining a Security Descriptor with the matching owner and group SIDs, and a DACL which contains ACEs for the owner, the group and for "Everyone", which represents what POSIX calls "others".

There's just one problem when trying to map the POSIX permission model onto the Windows permission model.

There's a leak in the definition of a "correct" ACL which disallows a certain POSIX permission setting. The official documentation explains in short the following:

- The requested permissions are checked against all ACEs of the user as well as all groups the user is member of. The permissions given in these user and groups access allowed ACEs are accumulated and the resulting set is the set of permissions of that user given for that object.
- The order of ACEs is important. The system reads them in sequence until either any single requested permission is denied or all requested permissions are granted. Reading stops when this condition is met. Later ACEs are not taken into account.

- All access denied ACEs **should** precede any access allowed ACE. ACLs following this rule are called "canonical".

Note that the last rule is a preference or a definition of correctness. It's not an absolute requirement. All Windows kernels will correctly deal with the ACL regardless of the order of allow and deny ACEs. The second rule is not modified to get the ACEs in the preferred order.

Unfortunately the security tab in the file properties dialog of the Windows Explorer insists to rearrange the order of the ACEs to canonical order before you can read them. Thank God, the sort order remains unchanged if one presses the Cancel button. But don't even **think** of pressing OK...

Canonical ACLs are unable to reflect each possible combination of POSIX permissions. Example:

```
rw-r-xrw-
```

Ok, so here's the first try to create a matching ACL, assuming the Windows permissions only have three bits, as their POSIX counterpart:

```
UserAllow:    110
GroupAllow:   101
OthersAllow:  110
```

Hmm, because of the accumulation of allow rights the user may execute because the group may execute.

Second try:

```
UserDeny:     001
GroupAllow:   101
OthersAllow:  110
```

Now the user may read and write but not execute. Better? No! Unfortunately the group may write now because others may write.

Third try:

```
UserDeny:     001
GroupDeny:    010
GroupAllow:   001
OthersAllow:  110
```

Now the group may not write as intended but unfortunately the user may not write anymore, either. How should this problem be solved? According to the canonical order a UserAllow has to follow the GroupDeny but it's easy to see that this can never be solved that way.

The only chance:

```
UserDeny:     001
UserAllow:    010
GroupDeny:    010
GroupAllow:   001
OthersAllow:  110
```

Again: This works on all existing versions of Windows NT, at the time of writing from at least Windows XP up to Server 2012 R2. Only the GUIs aren't able (or willing) to deal with that order.

3.6.4 Switching the user context

Since Windows XP, Windows users have been accustomed to the "Switch User" feature, which switches the entire desktop to another user while leaving the original user's desktop "suspended". Another Windows feature is the "Run as..." context menu entry, which allows you to start an application using another user account when right-clicking on applications and shortcuts.

On POSIX systems, this operation can be performed by processes running under the privileged user accounts (usually the "root" user account) on a per-process basis. This is called "switching the user context" for that process, and is performed using the POSIX **setuid** and **seteuid** system calls.

Synopsis

```
getconf [-v specification] variable_name [pathname]
getconf -a [pathname]
```

Options

```
-v specification     Indicate specific version for which configuration
                     values shall be fetched.
-a, --all            Print all known configuration values

Other options:

-h, --help           This text
-V, --version        Print program version and exit
```

Description

The **getconf** utility prints the value of the configuration variable specified by `variable_name`. If no `pathname` is given, **getconf** serves as a wrapper for the `confstr` and `sysconf` functions, supporting the symbolic constants defined in the `limits.h` and `unistd.h` headers, without their respective `_CS_` or `_SC_` prefixes.

If `pathname` is given, **getconf** prints the value of the configuration variable for the specified pathname. In this form, **getconf** serves as a wrapper for the `pathconf` function, supporting the symbolic constants defined in the `unistd.h` header, without the `_PC_` prefix.

If you specify the `-v` option, the parameter denotes a specification for which the value of the configuration variable should be printed. Note that the only specifications supported by Cygwin are `POSIX_V7_ILP32_OFFBIG` and the legacy `POSIX_V6_ILP32_OFFBIG` and `XBS5_ILP32_OFFBIG` equivalents.

Use the `-a` option to print a list of all available configuration variables for the system, or given `pathname`, and their values.

3.8.5   getfacl

getfacl — Display file and directory access control lists (ACLs)

Synopsis

```
getfacl [-adceEn] FILE [FILE2...]
```

Options

```
-a, --access         display the file access control list only
-d, --default        display the default access control list only
-c, --omit-header    do not display the comment header
-e, --all-effective  print all effective rights
-E, --no-effective   print no effective rights
-n, --numeric        print numeric user/group identifiers
-V, --version        print version and exit
-h, --help           this help text

When multiple files are specified on the command line, a blank
line separates the ACLs for each file.
```

Description

For each argument that is a regular file, special file or directory, **getfacl** displays the owner, the group, and the ACL. For directories **getfacl** displays additionally the default ACL. With no options specified, **getfacl** displays the filename, the owner, the group, the setuid (s), setgid (s), and sticky (t) bits if available, and both the ACL and the default ACL, if it exists. For more information on Cygwin and Windows ACLs, see Section 3.6 in the Cygwin User's Guide. The format for ACL output is as follows:

```
# file: filename
# owner: name or uid
# group: name or uid
# flags: sst
user::perm
user:name or uid:perm
group::perm
group:name or gid:perm
mask:perm
other:perm
default:user::perm
default:user:name or uid:perm
default:group::perm
default:group:name or gid:perm
default:mask:perm
default:other:perm
```

3.8.6   kill

kill — Send signals to processes

Synopsis

```
kill [-f] [-signal] [-s signal] pid1 [pid2 ...]
kill -l [signal]
```

Options

```
-f, --force      force, using win32 interface if necessary
-l, --list       print a list of signal names
-s, --signal     send signal (use kill --list for a list)
-h, --help       output usage information and exit
-V, --version    output version information and exit
```

Description

The **kill** program allows you to send arbitrary signals to other Cygwin programs. The usual purpose is to end a running program from some other window when ^C won't work, but you can also send program-specified signals such as SIGUSR1 to trigger actions within the program, like enabling debugging or re-opening log files. Each program defines the signals they understand.

You may need to specify the full path to use **kill** from within some shells, including **bash**, the default Cygwin shell. This is because **bash** defines a **kill** builtin function; see the **bash** man page under *BUILTIN COMMANDS* for more information. To make sure you are using the Cygwin version, try

```
$ /bin/kill --version
```

which should give the Cygwin **kill** version number and copyright information.

Unless you specific the `-f` option, the "pid" values used by **kill** are the Cygwin pids, not the Windows pids. To get a list of running programs and their Cygwin pids, use the Cygwin **ps** program. **ps -W** will display *all* windows pids.

The **kill -l** option prints the name of the given signal, or a list of all signal names if no signal is given.

To send a specific signal, use the `-signN` option, either with a signal number or a signal name (minus the "SIG" part), as shown in these examples:

Example 3.6 Using the kill command

```
$ kill 123
$ kill -1 123
$ kill -HUP 123
$ kill -f 123
```

Here is a list of available signals, their numbers, and some commentary on them, from the file `<sys/signal.h>`, which should be considered the official source of this information.

```
SIGHUP        1     hangup
SIGINT        2     interrupt
SIGQUIT       3     quit
SIGILL        4     illegal instruction (not reset when caught)
SIGTRAP       5     trace trap (not reset when caught)
SIGABRT       6     used by abort
SIGEMT        7     EMT instruction
SIGFPE        8     floating point exception
SIGKILL       9     kill (cannot be caught or ignored)
SIGBUS       10     bus error
SIGSEGV      11     segmentation violation
SIGSYS       12     bad argument to system call
SIGPIPE      13     write on a pipe with no one to read it
SIGALRM      14     alarm clock
SIGTERM      15     software termination signal from kill
SIGURG       16     urgent condition on IO channel
SIGSTOP      17     sendable stop signal not from tty
SIGTSTP      18     stop signal from tty
SIGCONT      19     continue a stopped process
SIGCHLD      20     to parent on child stop or exit
SIGCLD       20     System V name for SIGCHLD
SIGTTIN      21     to readers pgrp upon background tty read
SIGTTOU      22     like TTIN for output if (tp->t_local&LTOSTOP)
SIGIO        23     input/output possible
SIGPOLL      23     System V name for SIGIO
SIGXCPU      24     exceeded CPU time limit
SIGXFSZ      25     exceeded file size limit
SIGVTALRM    26     virtual time alarm
SIGPROF      27     profiling time alarm
SIGWINCH     28     window changed
SIGLOST      29     resource lost (eg, record-lock lost)
SIGPWR       29     power failure
SIGUSR1      30     user defined signal 1
SIGUSR2      31     user defined signal 2
```

3.8.7   ldd

ldd — Print shared library dependencies

Synopsis

```
ldd [OPTION]... FILE...
```

Options

```
-h, --help              print this help and exit
-V, --version           print version information and exit
-r, --function-relocs   process data and function relocations
                        (currently unimplemented)
-u, --unused            print unused direct dependencies
                        (currently unimplemented)
-v, --verbose           print all information
                        (currently unimplemented)
```

Description

ldd prints the shared libraries (DLLs) an executable or DLL is linked against. No modifying option is implemented yet.

3.8.8 locale

locale — Get locale-specific information

Synopsis

```
locale [-amvhV]
locale [-ck] NAME
locale [-usfnU]
```

Options

```
System information:

 -a, --all-locales   List all available supported locales
 -m, --charmaps      List all available character maps
 -v, --verbose       More verbose output

Modify output format:

 -c, --category-name List information about given category NAME
 -k, --keyword-name  Print information about given keyword NAME

Default locale information:

 -u, --user          Print locale of user's default UI language
 -s, --system        Print locale of system default UI language
 -f, --format        Print locale of user's regional format settings
                     (time, numeric & monetary)
 -n, --no-unicode    Print system default locale for non-Unicode programs
 -U, --utf           Attach \".UTF-8\" to the result

Other options:

 -h, --help          This text
 -V, --version       Print program version and exit
```

Description

locale without parameters prints information about the current locale environment settings.

The -u, -s, -f, and -n options can be used to request the various Windows locale settings. The purpose is to use this command in scripts to set the POSIX locale variables.

The -u option prints the current user's Windows UI locale to stdout. In Windows Vista and Windows 7 this setting is called the "Display Language"; there was no corresponding user setting in Windows XP. The -s option prints the systems default instead. The -f option prints the user's setting for time, date, number and currency. That's equivalent to the setting in the "Formats" or "Regional Options" tab in the "Region and Language" or "Regional and Language Options" dialog. With the -U option **locale** appends a ".UTF-8".

Usage example:

```
bash$ export LANG=$(locale -uU)
bash$ echo $LANG
en_US.UTF-8
bash$ export LC_TIME=$(locale -fU)
bash$ echo $LC_TIME
de_DE.UTF-8
```

The -a option is helpful to learn which locales are supported by your Windows machine. It prints all available locales and the allowed modifiers. Example:

```
bash$ locale -a
C
C.utf8
POSIX
af_ZA
af_ZA.utf8
am_ET
am_ET.utf8
...
be_BY
be_BY.utf8
be_BY@latin
...
ca_ES
ca_ES.utf8
ca_ES@euro
catalan
...
```

The -v option prints more detailed information about each available locale. Example:

```
bash$ locale -av
locale: af_ZA              archive: /cygdrive/c/Windows/system32/kernel32.dll
-------------------------------------------------------------------------------
 language | Afrikaans
territory | South Africa
  codeset | ISO-8859-1

locale: af_ZA.utf8         archive: /cygdrive/c/Windows/system32/kernel32.dll
-------------------------------------------------------------------------------
 language | Afrikaans
territory | South Africa
  codeset | UTF-8

...

locale: ca_ES@euro         archive: /cygdrive/c/Windows/system32/kernel32.dll
-------------------------------------------------------------------------------
```

```
 language | Catalan
territory | Spain
  codeset | ISO-8859-15

locale: catalan          archive: /usr/share/locale/locale.alias
----------------------------------------------------------------------
 language | Catalan
territory | Spain
  codeset | ISO-8859-1

...
```

The −m option prints the names of the available charmaps supported by Cygwin to stdout.

Otherwise, if arguments are given, **locale** prints the values assigned to these arguments. Arguments can be names of locale categories (for instance: LC_CTYPE, LC_MONETARY), or names of keywords supported in the locale categories (for instance: thousands_sep, charmap). The −c option prints additionally the name of the category. The −k option prints additionally the name of the keyword. Example:

```
bash$ locale -ck LC_MESSAGES
LC_MESSAGES
yesexpr="^[yY]"
noexpr="^[nN]"
yesstr="yes"
nostr="no"
messages-codeset="UTF-8"
bash$ locale noexpr
^[nN]
```

3.8.9 minidumper

minidumper — Write minidump from WIN32PID to FILENAME.dmp

Synopsis

```
minidumper [OPTION] FILENAME WIN32PID
```

Options

```
-t, --type     minidump type flags
-n, --nokill   don't terminate the dumped process
-d, --verbose  be verbose while dumping
-h, --help     output help information and exit
-q, --quiet    be quiet while dumping (default)
-V, --version  output version information and exit
```

Description

The **minidumper** utility can be used to create a minidump of a running Windows process. This minidump can be later analysed using breakpad or Windows debugging tools.

minidumper can be used with cygwin's Just-In-Time debugging facility in exactly the same way as **dumper** (See dumper(1)).

minidumper can also be started from the command line to create a minidump of any running process. For compatibility with **dumper** the target process is terminated after dumping unless the −n option is given.

3.8.10 mkgroup

mkgroup — Write /etc/group-like output to stdout

Synopsis

```
mkgroup [OPTION]...
```

Options

```
Options:

  -l,--local [machine]    Print local group accounts of \"machine\",
                          from local machine if no machine specified.
                          Automatically adding machine prefix for local
                          machine depends on settings in /etc/nsswitch.conf.
  -L,--Local machine      Ditto, but generate groupname with machine prefix.
  -d,--domain [domain]    Print domain groups,
                          from current domain if no domain specified.
  -c,--current            Print current group.
  -S,--separator char     For -L use character char as domain\\group
                          separator in groupname instead of default '+'.
  -o,--id-offset offset   Change the default offset (0x10000) added to gids
  -g,--group groupname    Only return information for the specified group.
                          One of -l, -d must be specified, too.
  -b,--no-builtin         Don't print BUILTIN groups.
  -U,--unix grouplist     Print UNIX groups when using -l on a UNIX Samba
                          server.  Grouplist is a comma-separated list of
                          groupnames or gid ranges (root,-25,50-100).
                          Enumerating large ranges can take a long time!
  -h,--help               Print this message.
  -v,--version            Print version information and exit.

Default is to print local groups on stand-alone machines, plus domain
groups on domain controllers and domain member machines.
```

Description

Don't use this command to generate a local /etc/group file, unless you really need one. See the Cygwin User's Guide for more information.

The **mkgroup** program can be used to create a local /etc/group file. Cygwin doesn't need this file, because it reads group information from the Windows account databases, but you can add an /etc/group file for instance, if your machine is often disconnected from its domain controller.

Note that this information is static, in contrast to the information automatically gathered by Cygwin from the Windows account databases. If you change the group information on your system, you'll need to regenerate the group file for it to have the new information.

By default, the information generated by **mkgroup** is equivalent to the information generated by Cygwin itself. The -d and -l/-L options allow you to specify where the information comes from, some domain, or the local SAM of a machine. Note that you can only enumerate accounts from trusted domains. Any non-trusted domain will be ignored. Access-restrictions of your current account apply. The -l/-L when used with a machine name, tries to contact that machine to enumerate local groups of other machines, typically outside of domains. This scenario cannot be covered by Cygwin's account automatism. If you want to use the -L option, but you don't like the default domain/group separator from /etc/nsswitch.conf, you can specify another separator using the -S option, for instance:

Example 3.7 Setting up group entry for current user with different domain/group separator

```
$ mkgroup -L server1 -S= > /etc/group
```

For very simple needs, an entry for the current user's group can be created by using the option -c.

The -o option allows for (unlikely) special cases with multiple machines where the GIDs might match otherwise. The -g option only prints the information for one group. The -U option allows you to enumerate the standard UNIX groups on a Samba machine. It's used together with -l samba-server or -L samba-server. The normal UNIX groups are usually not enumerated, but they can show up as a group in **ls -l** output.

3.8.11   mkpasswd

mkpasswd — Write /etc/passwd-like output to stdout

Synopsis

```
mkpasswd [OPTIONS]...
```

Options

```
   Options:

   -l,--local [machine]    Print local user accounts of \"machine\",
                           from local machine if no machine specified.
                           Automatically adding machine prefix for local
                           machine depends on settings in /etc/nsswitch.conf.
   -L,--Local machine      Ditto, but generate username with machine prefix.
   -d,--domain [domain]    Print domain accounts,
                           from current domain if no domain specified.
   -c,--current            Print current user.
   -S,--separator char     For -L use character char as domain\\user
                           separator in username instead of the default '+'.
   -o,--id-offset offset   Change the default offset (0x10000) added to uids
                           of foreign local machine accounts.  Use with -l/-L.
   -u,--username username  Only return information for the specified user.
                           One of -l, -d must be specified, too
   -b,--no-builtin         Don't print BUILTIN users.
   -p,--path-to-home path  Use specified path instead of user account home dir
                           or /home prefix.
   -U,--unix userlist      Print UNIX users when using -l on a UNIX Samba
                           server.  Userlist is a comma-separated list of
                           usernames or uid ranges (root,-25,50-100).
                           Enumerating large ranges can take a long time!
   -h,--help               Displays this message.
   -V,--version            Version information and exit.

Default is to print local accounts on stand-alone machines, domain accounts
on domain controllers and domain member machines.
```

Description

Don't use this command to generate a local /etc/passwd file, unless you really need one. See the Cygwin User's Guide for more information.

The **mkpasswd** program can be used to create a /etc/passwd file. Cygwin doesn't need this file, because it reads user information from the Windows account databases, but you can add an /etc/passwd file, for instance if your machine is often disconnected from its domain controller.

Note that this information is static, in contrast to the information automatically gathered by Cygwin from the Windows account databases. If you change the user information on your system, you'll need to regenerate the passwd file for it to have the new information.

By default, the information generated by **mkpasswd** is equivalent to the information generated by Cygwin itself. The −d and −l/−L options allow you to specify where the information comes from, some domain, or the local SAM of a machine. Note that you can only enumerate accounts from trusted domains. Any non-trusted domain will be ignored. Access-restrictions of your current account apply. The −l/−L when used with a machine name, tries to contact that machine to enumerate local groups of other machines, typically outside of domains. This scenario cannot be covered by Cygwin's account automatism. If you want to use the −L option, but you don't like the default domain/group separator from /etc/nsswitch.conf, you can specify another separator using the −S option, analog to **mkgroup**.

For very simple needs, an entry for the current user can be created by using the option −c.

The −o option allows for special cases (such as multiple domains) where the UIDs might match otherwise. The −p option causes **mkpasswd** to use the specified prefix instead of the account home dir or /home/. For example, this command:

Example 3.8 Using an alternate home root

```
$ mkpasswd -l -p "$(cygpath -H)" > /etc/passwd
```

---

would put local users' home directories in the Windows 'Profiles' directory. The −u option creates just an entry for the specified user. The −U option allows you to enumerate the standard UNIX users on a Samba machine. It's used together with −l samba-server or −L samba-server. The normal UNIX users are usually not enumerated, but they can show up as file owners in **ls -l** output.

3.8.12 mount

mount — Display information about mounted filesystems, or mount a filesystem

Synopsis

```
mount [OPTION] [<win32path> <posixpath>]
mount -a
mount <posixpath>
```

Options

```
-a, --all                     mount all filesystems mentioned in fstab
-c, --change-cygdrive-prefix  change the cygdrive path prefix to <posixpath>
-f, --force                   force mount, don't warn about missing mount
                              point directories
-h, --help                    output usage information and exit
-m, --mount-entries           write fstab entries to replicate mount points
                              and cygdrive prefixes
-o, --options X[,X...]        specify mount options
-p, --show-cygdrive-prefix    show user and/or system cygdrive path prefix
-V, --version                 output version information and exit
```

Description

The **mount** program is used to map your drives and shares onto Cygwin's simulated POSIX directory tree, much like as is done by mount commands on typical UNIX systems. However, in contrast to mount points given in /etc/fstab, mount points created or changed with **mount** are not persistent. They disappear immediately after the last process of the current user exited. Please see Section 3.1.2 for more information on the concepts behind the Cygwin POSIX file system and strategies for using mounts. To remove mounts temporarily, use **umount**

Using mount

If you just type **mount** with no parameters, it will display the current mount table for you.

Example 3.9 Displaying the current set of mount points

```
$ mount
C:/cygwin/bin on /usr/bin type ntfs (binary)
C:/cygwin/lib on /usr/lib type ntfs (binary)
C:/cygwin on / type ntfs (binary)
C: on /mnt/c type ntfs (binary,user,noumount)
D: on /mnt/d type fat (binary,user,noumount)
```

In this example, c:/cygwin is the POSIX root and the D drive is mapped to /mnt/d. Note that in this case, the root mount is a system-wide mount point that is visible to all users running Cygwin programs, whereas the /mnt/d mount is only visible to the current user.

The **mount** utility is also the mechanism for adding new mounts to the mount table in memory. The following example demonstrates how to mount the directory //pollux/home/joe/data to /data for the duration of the current session.

Example 3.10 Adding mount points

```
$ ls /data
ls: /data: No such file or directory
$ mount //pollux/home/joe/data /data
mount: warning - /data does not exist!
$ mount
//pollux/home/joe/data on /data type smbfs (binary)
C:/cygwin/bin on /usr/bin type ntfs (binary)
C:/cygwin/lib on /usr/lib type ntfs (binary)
C:/cygwin on / type ntfs (binary)
C: on /c type ntfs (binary,user,noumount)
D: on /d type fat (binary,user,noumount)
```

A given POSIX path may only exist once in the mount table. Attempts to replace the mount will fail with a busy error. The -f (force) option causes the old mount to be silently replaced with the new one, provided the old mount point was a user mount point. It's not valid to replace system-wide mount points. Additionally, the -f option will silence warnings about the non-existence of directories at the Win32 path location.

The -o option is the method via which various options about the mount point may be recorded. The following options are available (note that most of the options are duplicates of other mount flags):

```
  acl         - Use the filesystem's access control lists (ACLs) to
                implement real POSIX permissions (default).
  binary      - Files default to binary mode (default).
  bind        - Allows to remount part of the file hierarchy somewhere else.
                Different from other mount calls, the first argument
                specifies an absolute POSIX path, rather than a Win32 path.
                This POSIX path is remounted to the POSIX path specified as
                the second parameter.  The conversion to a Win32 path is done
                within Cygwin immediately at the time of the call.  Note that
                symlinks are ignored while performing this path conversion.
```

```
cygexec    - Treat all files below mount point as cygwin executables.
dos        - Always convert leading spaces and trailing dots and spaces to
             characters in the UNICODE private use area.  This allows to use
             broken filesystems which only allow DOS filenames, even if they
             are not recognized as such by Cygwin.
exec       - Treat all files below mount point as executable.
ihash      - Always fake inode numbers rather than using the ones returned
             by the filesystem.  This allows to use broken filesystems which
             don't return unambiguous inode numbers, even if they are not
             recognized as such by Cygwin.
noacl      - Ignore ACLs and fake POSIX permissions.
nosuid     - No suid files are allowed (currently unimplemented)
notexec    - Treat all files below mount point as not executable.
override   - Override immutable mount points.
posix=0    - Switch off case sensitivity for paths under this mount point.
posix=1    - Switch on case sensitivity for paths under this mount point
             (default).
sparse     - Switch on support for sparse files.  This option only makes
             sense on NTFS and then only if you really need sparse files.
text       - Files default to CRLF text mode line endings.
```

For a more complete description of the mount options and the /etc/fstab file, see Section 3.1.2.

Note that all mount points added with **mount** are user mount points. System mount points can only be specified in the /etc/fstab file.

If you added mount points to /etc/fstab or your /etc/fstab.d/<username> file, you can add these mount points to your current user session using the -a/--all option, or by specifing the posix path alone on the command line. As an example, consider you added a mount point with the POSIX path /my/mount. You can add this mount point with either one of the following two commands to your current user session.

```
$ mount /my/mount
$ mount -a
```

The first command just adds the /my/mount mount point to your current session, the **mount -a** adds all new mount points to your user session.

If you change a mount point to point to another native path, or if you changed the flags of a mount point, you have to **umount** the mount point first, before you can add it again. Please note that all such added mount points are added as user mount points, and that the rule that system mount points can't be removed or replaced in a running session still applies.

To bind a POSIX path to another POSIX path, use the bind mount flag.

```
$ mount -o bind /var /usr/var
```

This command makes the file hirarchy under /var additionally available under /usr/var.

The -m option causes the **mount** utility to output the current mount table in a series of fstab entries. You can save this output as a backup when experimenting with the mount table. Copy the output to /etc/fstab to restore the old state. It also makes moving your settings to a different machine much easier.

Cygdrive mount points

Whenever Cygwin cannot use any of the existing mounts to convert from a particular Win32 path to a POSIX one, Cygwin will, instead, convert to a POSIX path using a default mount point: /cygdrive. For example, if Cygwin accesses z:\foo and the z drive is not currently in the mount table, then z:\ will be accessible as /cygdrive/z. The **mount** utility can be used to change this default automount prefix through the use of the "--change-cygdrive-prefix" option. In the following example, we will set the automount prefix to /mnt:

Example 3.11 Changing the default prefix

```
$ mount --change-cygdrive-prefix /mnt
```

Note that the cygdrive prefix can be set both per-user and system-wide, and that as with all mounts, a user-specific mount takes precedence over the system-wide setting. The **mount** utility creates system-wide mounts by default if you do not specify a type. You can always see the user and system cygdrive prefixes with the -p option. Using the --options flag with --change-cygdrive-prefix makes all new automounted filesystems default to this set of options. For instance (using the short form of the command line flags)

Example 3.12 Changing the default prefix with specific mount options

```
$ mount -c /mnt -o binary,noacl
```

Limitations

Limitations: there is a hard-coded limit of 64 mount points (up to Cygwin 1.7.9: 30 mount points). Also, although you can mount to pathnames that do not start with "/", there is no way to make use of such mount points.

Normally the POSIX mount point in Cygwin is an existing empty directory, as in standard UNIX. If this is the case, or if there is a place-holder for the mount point (such as a file, a symbolic link pointing anywhere, or a non-empty directory), you will get the expected behavior. Files present in a mount point directory before the mount become invisible to Cygwin programs.

It is sometimes desirable to mount to a non-existent directory, for example to avoid cluttering the root directory with names such as a, b, c pointing to disks. Although **mount** will give you a warning, most everything will work properly when you refer to the mount point explicitly. Some strange effects can occur however. For example if your current working directory is /dir, say, and /dir/mtpt is a mount point, then mtpt will not show up in an **ls** or **echo** * command and **find .** will not find mtpt.

3.8.13   passwd

passwd — Change USER's password or password attributes.

Synopsis

```
passwd [OPTION] [USER]
```

Options

```
User operations:
  -l, --lock                lock USER's account.
  -u, --unlock              unlock USER's account.
  -c, --cannot-change       USER can't change password.
  -C, --can-change          USER can change password.
  -e, --never-expires       USER's password never expires.
  -E, --expires             USER's password expires according to system's
                            password aging rule.
  -p, --pwd-not-required    no password required for USER.
  -P, --pwd-required        password is required for USER.
  -R, --reg-store-pwd       enter password to store it in the registry for
                            later usage by services to be able to switch
                            to this user context with network credentials.

System operations:
  -i, --inactive NUM        set NUM of days before inactive accounts are disabled
```

```
                              (inactive accounts are those with expired passwords).
  -n, --minage MINDAYS        set system minimum password age to MINDAYS days.
  -x, --maxage MAXDAYS        set system maximum password age to MAXDAYS days.
  -L, --length LEN            set system minimum password length to LEN.

Other options:
  -d, --logonserver SERVER    connect to SERVER (e.g. domain controller).
                              Usually not required.
  -S, --status                display password status for USER (locked, expired,
                              etc.) plus global system password settings.
  -h, --help                  output usage information and exit.
  -V, --version               output version information and exit.

If no option is given, change USER's password.  If no user name is given,
operate on current user.  System operations must not be mixed with user
operations.  Don't specify a USER when triggering a system operation.

Don't specify a user or any other option together with the -R option.
Non-Admin users can only store their password if cygserver is running.
Note that storing even obfuscated passwords in the registry is not overly
secure.  Use this feature only if the machine is adequately locked down.
Don't use this feature if you don't need network access within a remote
session.  You can delete your stored password by using `passwd -R' and
specifying an empty password.
```

Description

passwd changes passwords for user accounts. A normal user may only change the password for their own account, but administrators may change passwords on any account. **passwd** also changes account information, such as password expiry dates and intervals.

For password changes, the user is first prompted for their old password, if one is present. This password is then encrypted and compared against the stored password. The user has only one chance to enter the correct password. The administrators are permitted to bypass this step so that forgotten passwords may be changed.

The user is then prompted for a replacement password. **passwd** will prompt twice for this replacement and compare the second entry against the first. Both entries are required to match in order for the password to be changed.

After the password has been entered, password aging information is checked to see if the user is permitted to change their password at this time. If not, **passwd** refuses to change the password and exits.

To get current password status information, use the -S option. Administrators can use **passwd** to perform several account maintenance functions (users may perform some of these functions on their own accounts). Accounts may be locked with the -l flag and unlocked with the -u flag. Similarly, -c disables a user's ability to change passwords, and -C allows a user to change passwords. For password expiry, the -e option disables expiration, while the -E option causes the password to expire according to the system's normal aging rules. Use -p to disable the password requirement for a user, or -P to require a password.

Administrators can also use **passwd** to change system-wide password expiry and length requirements with the -i, -n, -x, and -L options. The -i option is used to disable an account after the password has been expired for a number of days. After a user account has had an expired password for *NUM* days, the user may no longer sign on to the account. The -n option is used to set the minimum number of days before a password may be changed. The user will not be permitted to change the password until *MINDAYS* days have elapsed. The -x option is used to set the maximum number of days a password remains valid. After *MAXDAYS* days, the password is required to be changed. Allowed values for the above options are 0 to 999. The -L option sets the minimum length of allowed passwords for users who don't belong to the administrators group to *LEN* characters. Allowed values for the minimum password length are 0 to 14. In any of the above cases, a value of 0 means `no restrictions'.

All operations affecting the current user are by default run against the logon server of the current user (taken from the environment variable LOGONSERVER. When password or account information of other users should be changed, the logon server is evaluated automatically. In rare cases, it might be necessary to switch to another domain controller to perform the action. In this case, use the -d option to specify the machine to run the command against. Note that the current user must have account operator permissions to perform user account changes in a domain.

Users can use the **passwd -R** to enter a password which then gets stored in a special area of the registry on the local system, which is also used by Windows to store passwords of accounts running Windows services. When a privileged Cygwin application calls the **set{e}uid(user_id)** system call, Cygwin checks if a password for that user has been stored in this registry area. If so, it uses this password to switch to this user account using that password. This allows you to logon through, for instance, **ssh** with public key authentication and get a full qualified user token with all credentials for network access. However, the method has some drawbacks security-wise. This is explained in more detail in Section 3.6.

Please note that storing passwords in that registry area is a privileged operation which only administrative accounts are allowed to do. Administrators can enter the password for other user accounts into the registry by specifying the username on the commandline. If normal, non-admin users should be allowed to enter their passwords using **passwd -R**, it's required to run **cygserver** as a service under the LocalSystem account before running **passwd -R**. This only affects storing passwords. Using passwords in privileged processes does not require **cygserver** to run.

Limitations: Users may not be able to change their password on some systems.

3.8.14 pldd

pldd — List dynamic shared objects loaded into a process

Synopsis

```
pldd [OPTION...] PID
```

Options

```
-?, --help              Give this help list
    --usage             Give a short usage message
-V, --version           Print program version
```

Description

pldd prints the shared libraries (DLLs) loaded by the process with the given PID.

3.8.15 ps

ps — Report process status

Synopsis

```
ps [-aefls] [-u UID]
```

Options

```
-a, --all       show processes of all users
-e, --everyone  show processes of all users
-f, --full      show process uids, ppids
-h, --help      output usage information and exit
-l, --long      show process uids, ppids, pgids, winpids
-p, --process   show information for specified PID
-s, --summary   show process summary
-u, --user      list processes owned by UID
-V, --version   output version information and exit
-W, --windows   show windows as well as cygwin processes
With no options, ps outputs the long format by default
```

Description

The **ps** program gives the status of all the Cygwin processes running on the system (ps = "process status"). Due to the limitations of simulating a POSIX environment under Windows, there is little information to give.

The PID column is the process ID you need to give to the **kill** command. The PPID is the parent process ID, and PGID is the process group ID. The WINPID column is the process ID displayed by NT's Task Manager program. The TTY column gives which pseudo-terminal a process is running on, or a ' ? ' for services. The UID column shows which user owns each process. STIME is the time the process was started, and COMMAND gives the name of the program running. Listings may also have a status flag in column zero; S means stopped or suspended (in other words, in the background), I means waiting for input or interactive (foreground), and O means waiting to output.

By default, **ps** will only show processes owned by the current user. With either the −a or −e option, all user's processes (and system processes) are listed. There are historical UNIX reasons for the synonomous options, which are functionally identical. The −f option outputs a "full" listing with usernames for UIDs. The −l option is the default display mode, showing a "long" listing with all the above columns. The other display option is −s, which outputs a shorter listing of just PID, TTY, STIME, and COMMAND. The −u option allows you to show only processes owned by a specific user. The −p option allows you to show information for only the process with the specified PID. The −W option causes **ps** show non-Cygwin Windows processes as well as Cygwin processes. The WINPID is also the PID, and they can be killed with the Cygwin **kill** command's −f option.

3.8.16   regtool

regtool — View or edit the Windows registry

Synopsis

```
regtool [OPTION] (add|check|get|list|remove|unset|load|unload|save) KEY
```

Options

```
Actions:

  add KEY\SUBKEY              add new SUBKEY
  check KEY                   exit 0 if KEY exists, 1 if not
  get KEY\VALUE               prints VALUE to stdout
  list KEY                    list SUBKEYs and VALUEs
  remove KEY                  remove KEY
  set KEY\VALUE [data ...]    set VALUE
  unset KEY\VALUE             removes VALUE from KEY
  load KEY\SUBKEY PATH        load hive from PATH into new SUBKEY
  unload KEY\SUBKEY           unload hive and remove SUBKEY
  save KEY\SUBKEY PATH        save SUBKEY into new file PATH
  restore KEY\SUBKEY PATH     restore SUBKEY from file PATH

Options for 'list' Action:

  -k, --keys                 print only KEYs
  -l, --list                 print only VALUEs
  -p, --postfix              like ls -p, appends '\' postfix to KEY names

Options for 'get' Action:

  -b, --binary               print REG_BINARY data as hex bytes
  -n, --none                 print data as stream of bytes as stored in registry
  -x, --hex                  print numerical data as hex numbers

Options for 'set' Action:
```

```
-b, --binary          set type to REG_BINARY (hex args or '-')
-D, --dword-be        set type to REG_DWORD_BIG_ENDIAN
-e, --expand-string   set type to REG_EXPAND_SZ
-i, --integer         set type to REG_DWORD
-m, --multi-string    set type to REG_MULTI_SZ
-n, --none            set type to REG_NONE
-Q, --qword           set type to REG_QWORD
-s, --string          set type to REG_SZ

Options for 'set' and 'unset' Actions:

-K<c>, --key-separator[=]<c>  set key separator to <c> instead of '\'

Options for 'restore' action:

-f, --force   restore even if open handles exist at or beneath the location
              in the registry hierarchy to which KEY\SUBKEY points

Other Options:

-h, --help     output usage information and exit
-q, --quiet    no error output, just nonzero return if KEY/VALUE missing
-v, --verbose  verbose output, including VALUE contents when applicable
-w, --wow64    access 64 bit registry view (ignored on 32 bit Windows)
-W, --wow32    access 32 bit registry view (ignored on 32 bit Windows)
-V, --version  output version information and exit

KEY is in the format [host]\prefix\KEY\KEY\VALUE, where host is optional
remote host in either \\hostname or hostname: format and prefix is any of:
  root    HKCR  HKEY_CLASSES_ROOT (local only)
  config  HKCC  HKEY_CURRENT_CONFIG (local only)
  user    HKCU  HKEY_CURRENT_USER (local only)
  machine HKLM  HKEY_LOCAL_MACHINE
  users   HKU   HKEY_USERS

You can use forward slash ('/') as a separator instead of backslash, in
that case backslash is treated as escape character
Example: regtool get '\user\software\Microsoft\Clock\iFormat'
```

Description

The **regtool** program allows shell scripts to access and modify the Windows registry. Note that modifying the Windows registry is dangerous, and carelessness here can result in an unusable system. Be careful.

The -v option means "verbose". For most commands, this causes additional or lengthier messages to be printed. Conversely, the -q option supresses error messages, so you can use the exit status of the program to detect if a key exists or not (for example).

The -w option allows you to access the 64 bit view of the registry. Several subkeys exist in a 32 bit and a 64 bit version when running on Windows 64. Since Cygwin is running in 32 bit mode, it only has access to the 32 bit view of these registry keys. When using the -w switch, the 64 bit view is used and **regtool** can access the entire registry. This option is simply ignored when running on 32 bit Windows versions.

The -W option allows you to access the 32 bit view on the registry. The purpose of this option is mainly for symmetry. It permits creation of OS agnostic scripts which would also work in a hypothetical 64 bit version of Cygwin.

You must provide **regtool** with an *action* following options (if any). Currently, the action must be add, set, check, get, list, remove, set, or unset.

The add action adds a new key. The check action checks to see if a key exists (the exit code of the program is zero if it does, nonzero if it does not). The get action gets the value of a key, and prints it (and nothing else) to stdout. Note: if the value doesn't exist, an error message is printed and the program returns a non-zero exit code. If you give -q, it doesn't print the message but does return the non-zero exit code.

The list action lists the subkeys and values belonging to the given key. With list, the -k option instructs **regtool** to print only KEYs, and the -l option to print only VALUEs. The -p option postfixes a '/' to each KEY, but leave VALUEs with no postfix. The remove action removes a key. Note that you may need to remove everything in the key before you may remove it, but don't rely on this stopping you from accidentally removing too much.

The get action prints a value within a key. With the -b option, data is printed as hex bytes. -n allows to print the data as a typeless stream of bytes. Integer values (REG_DWORD, REG_QWORD) are usually printed as decimal values. The -x option allows to print the numbers as hexadecimal values.

The set action sets a value within a key. -b means it's binary data (REG_BINARY). The binary values are specified as hex bytes in the argument list. If the argument is '-', binary data is read from stdin instead. -d or -i means the value is a 32 bit integer value (REG_DWORD). -D means the value is a 32 bit integer value in Big Endian representation (REG_DWORD_BIG_ENDIAN). -Q means the value is a 64 bit integer value (REG_QWORD). -s means the value is a string (REG_SZ). -e means it's an expanding string (REG_EXPAND_SZ) that contains embedded environment variables. -m means it's a multi-string (REG_MULTI_SZ). If you don't specify one of these, **regtool** tries to guess the type based on the value you give. If it looks like a number, it's a DWORD, unless it's value doesn't fit into 32 bit, in which case it's a QWORD. If it starts with a percent, it's an expanding string. If you give multiple values, it's a multi-string. Else, it's a regular string.

The unset action removes a value from a key.

The load action adds a new subkey and loads the contents of a registry hive into it. The parent key must be HKEY_LOCAL_MACHINE or HKEY_USERS. The unload action unloads the file and removes the subkey.

The save action saves a subkey into a registry file. Ideally you append the suffix .reg to the file so it gets automatically recognized as registry file by **Windows Explorer**.

The restore action restores a registry subkey from a file saved via the aforementioned save action.

By default, the last "\" or "/" is assumed to be the separator between the key and the value. You can use the -K option to provide an alternate key/value separator character.

3.8.17 setfacl

setfacl — Modify file and directory access control lists (ACLs)

Synopsis

```
setfacl [-n] {-f ACL_FILE | -s acl_entries} FILE...
setfacl [-n] {[-bk]|[-x acl_entries] [-m acl_entries]} FILE...
```

Options

```
-b, --remove-all        remove all extended ACL entries\n"
-x, --delete            delete one or more specified ACL entries\n"
-f, --file              set ACL entries for FILE to ACL entries read\n"
                        from ACL_FILE\n"
-k, --remove-default    remove all default ACL entries\n"
-m, --modify            modify one or more specified ACL entries\n"
-n, --no-mask           don't recalculate the effective rights mask\n"
    --mask              do recalculate the effective rights mask\n"
-s, --set               set specified ACL entries on FILE\n"
-V, --version           print version and exit\n"
-h, --help              this help text\n"

At least one of (-b, -x, -f, -k, -m, -s) must be specified\n"
```

Description

For each file given as parameter, **setfacl** will either replace its complete ACL (-s, -f), or it will add, modify, or delete ACL entries. For more information on Cygwin and Windows ACLs, see Section 3.6 in the Cygwin User's Guide.

Acl_entries are one or more comma-separated ACL entries from the following list:

```
u[ser]::perm
u[ser]:uid:perm
g[roup]::perm
g[roup]:gid:perm
m[ask]::perm
o[ther]::perm
```

Default entries are like the above with the additional default identifier. For example:

```
d[efault]:u[ser]:uid:perm
```

perm is either a 3-char permissions string in the form "rwx" with the character ' – ' for no permission or it is the octal representation of the permissions, a value from 0 (equivalent to "---") to 7 ("rwx"). *uid* is a user name or a numerical uid. *gid* is a group name or a numerical gid.

The following options are supported:

-b,--remove-all Remove all extended ACL entries. The base ACL entries of the owner, group and others are retained. This option can be combined with the -k,--remove-default option to delete all non-standard POSIX permissions.

-x,--delete Delete one or more specified entries from the file's ACL. The owner, group and others entries must not be deleted. Acl_entries to be deleted should be specified without permissions, as in the following list:

```
u[ser]:uid[:]
g[roup]:gid[:]
m[ask][:]
d[efault]:u[ser][:uid]
d[efault]:g[roup][:gid]
d[efault]:m[ask][:]
d[efault]:o[ther][:]
```

-f,--file Take the Acl_entries from ACL_FILE one per line. Whitespace characters are ignored, and the character "#" may be used to start a comment. The special filename "-" indicates reading from stdin. Note that you can use this with **getfacl** and **setfacl** to copy ACLs from one file to another:

```
$ getfacl source_file | setfacl -f - target_file
```

Required entries are: one user entry for the owner of the file, one group entry for the group of the file, and one other entry.

If additional user and group entries are given: a mask entry for the file group class of the file, and no duplicate user or group entries with the same uid/gid.

If it is a directory: one default user entry for the owner of the file, one default group entry for the group of the file, one default mask entry for the file group class, and one default other entry.

-k,--remove-default Remove all default ACL entries. If no default ACL entries exist, no warnings are issued. This option can be combined with the -b,--remove-all option to delete all non-standard POSIX permissions.

-m,--modify Add or modify one or more specified ACL entries. Acl_entries is a comma-separated list of entries from the same list as above.

-n,--no-mask Valid in conjunction with -m. Do not recalculate the effective rights mask. The default behavior of setfacl is to recalculate the ACL mask entry, unless a mask entry was explicitly given. The mask entry is set to the union of all permissions of the owning group, and all named user and group entries. (These are exactly the entries affected by the mask entry).

--mask Valid in conjunction with -m. Do recalculate the effective rights mask, even if an ACL mask entry was explicitly given. (See the -n option.)

-s,--set Like -f, but set the file's ACL with Acl_entries specified in a comma-separated list on the command line.

While the -x and -m options may be used in the same command, the -f and -s options may be used only exclusively.

Directories may contain default ACL entries. Files created in a directory that contains default ACL entries will have permissions according to the combination of the current umask, the explicit permissions requested and the default ACL entries.

3.8.18 setmetamode

setmetamode — Get or set keyboard meta mode

Synopsis

```
setmetamode [metabit|escprefix]
```

Options

```
  Without argument, it shows the current meta key mode.

  metabit|meta|bit      The meta key sets the top bit of the character.
  escprefix|esc|prefix  The meta key sends an escape prefix.

Other options:

  -h, --help            This text
  -V, --version         Print program version and exit
```

Description

setmetamode can be used to determine and set the key code sent by the meta (aka Alt) key.

3.8.19 ssp

ssp — Single-step profile COMMAND

Synopsis

```
ssp [options] low_pc high_pc command...
```

Options

```
  -c, --console-trace   trace every EIP value to the console. *Lots* slower.
  -d, --disable         disable single-stepping by default; use
                        OutputDebugString ("ssp on") to enable stepping
  -e, --enable          enable single-stepping by default; use
                        OutputDebugString ("ssp off") to disable stepping
  -h, --help            output usage information and exit
  -l, --dll             enable dll profiling.  A chart of relative DLL usage
                        is produced after the run.
  -s, --sub-threads     trace sub-threads too.  Dangerous if you have
                        race conditions.
  -t, --trace-eip       trace every EIP value to a file TRACE.SSP.  This
```

```
                              gets big *fast*.
  -v, --verbose               output verbose messages about debug events.
  -V, --version               output version information and exit

Example: ssp 0x401000 0x403000 hello.exe
```

Description

SSP - The Single Step Profiler

Original Author: DJ Delorie

The SSP is a program that uses the Win32 debug API to run a program one ASM instruction at a time. It records the location of each instruction used, how many times that instruction is used, and all function calls. The results are saved in a format that is usable by the profiling program **gprof**, although **gprof** will claim the values are seconds, they really are instruction counts. More on that later.

Because the SSP was originally designed to profile the Cygwin DLL, it does not automatically select a block of code to report statistics on. You must specify the range of memory addresses to keep track of manually, but it's not hard to figure out what to specify. Use the "objdump" program to determine the bounds of the target's ".text" section. Let's say we're profiling cygwin1.dll. Make sure you've built it with debug symbols (else **gprof** won't run) and run objdump like this:

```
$ objdump -h cygwin1.dll
```

It will print a report like this:

```
cygwin1.dll:        file format pei-i386

Sections:
Idx Name            Size      VMA       LMA       File off  Algn
  0 .text           0007ea00  61001000  61001000  00000400  2**2
                    CONTENTS, ALLOC, LOAD, READONLY, CODE, DATA
  1 .data           00008000  61080000  61080000  0007ee00  2**2
                    CONTENTS, ALLOC, LOAD, DATA
  . . .
```

The only information we're concerned with are the VMA of the .text section and the VMA of the section after it (sections are usually contiguous; you can also add the Size to the VMA to get the end address). In this case, the VMA is 0x61001000 and the ending address is either 0x61080000 (start of .data method) or 0x0x6107fa00 (VMA+Size method).

There are two basic ways to use SSP - either profiling a whole program, or selectively profiling parts of the program.

To profile a whole program, just run **ssp** without options. By default, it will step the whole program. Here's a simple example, using the numbers above:

```
$ ssp 0x61001000 0x61080000 hello.exe
```

This will step the whole program. It will take at least 8 minutes on a PII/300 (yes, really). When it's done, it will create a file called "gmon.out". You can turn this data file into a readable report with **gprof**:

```
$ gprof -b cygwin1.dll
```

The "-b" means 'skip the help pages'. You can omit this until you're familiar with the report layout. The **gprof** documentation explains a lot about this report, but **ssp** changes a few things. For example, the first part of the report reports the amount of time spent in each function, like this:

```
Each sample counts as 0.01 seconds.
  %   cumulative   self              self     total
 time   seconds   seconds    calls  ms/call  ms/call  name
 10.02   231.22     72.43       46  1574.57  1574.57  strcspn
  7.95   288.70     57.48      130   442.15   442.15  strncasematch
```

The "seconds" columns are really CPU opcodes, 1/100 second per opcode. So, "231.22" above means 23,122 opcodes. The ms/call values are 10x too big; 1574.57 means 157.457 opcodes per call. Similar adjustments need to be made for the "self" and "children" columns in the second part of the report.

OK, so now we've got a huge report that took a long time to generate, and we've identified a spot we want to work on optimizing. Let's say it's the time() function. We can use SSP to selectively profile this function by using OutputDebugString() to control SSP from within the program. Here's a sample program:

```
#include <windows.h>
main()
{
    time_t t;
    OutputDebugString("ssp on");
    time(&t);
    OutputDebugString("ssp off");
}
```

Then, add the −d option to ssp to default to *disabling* profiling. The program will run at full speed until the first OutputDebugString, then step until the second. You can then use **gprof** (as usual) to see the performance profile for just that portion of the program's execution.

There are many options to ssp. Since step-profiling makes your program run about 1,000 times slower than normal, it's best to understand all the options so that you can narrow down the parts of your program you need to single-step.

−v - verbose. This prints messages about threads starting and stopping, OutputDebugString calls, DLLs loading, etc.

−t and −c - tracing. With −t, *every* step's address is written to the file "trace.ssp". This can be used to help debug functions, since it can trace multiple threads. Clever use of scripts can match addresses with disassembled opcodes if needed. Warning: creates *huge* files, very quickly. −c prints each address to the console, useful for debugging key chunks of assembler. Use add r2line −C −f −s −e foo.exe < trace.ssp > lines.ssp and then perl cvttrace to convert to symbolic traces.

−s - subthreads. Usually, you only need to trace the main thread, but sometimes you need to trace all threads, so this enables that. It's also needed when you want to profile a function that only a subthread calls. However, using OutputDebugString automatically enables profiling on the thread that called it, not the main thread.

−l - dll profiling. Generates a pretty table of how much time was spent in each dll the program used. No sense optimizing a function in your program if most of the time is spent in the DLL. I usually use the −v, −s, and −l options:

```
$ ssp −v −s −l −d 0x61001000 0x61080000 hello.exe
```

3.8.20   strace

strace — Trace system calls and signals

Synopsis

```
strace [OPTIONS] <command-line>
strace [OPTIONS] -p <pid>
```

Options

```
-b, --buffer-size=SIZE      set size of output file buffer
-d, --no-delta              don't display the delta-t microsecond timestamp
-e, --events                log all Windows DEBUG_EVENTS (toggle - default true)
-f, --trace-children        trace child processes (toggle - default true)
-h, --help                  output usage information and exit
-m, --mask=MASK             set message filter mask
```

```
-n, --crack-error-numbers      output descriptive text instead of error
                               numbers for Windows errors
-o, --output=FILENAME          set output file to FILENAME
-p, --pid=n                    attach to executing program with cygwin pid n
-q, --quiet                    toggle "quiet" flag.  Defaults to on if "-p",
                               off otherwise.
-S, --flush-period=PERIOD      flush buffered strace output every PERIOD secs
-t, --timestamp                use an absolute hh:mm:ss timestamp insted of
                               the default microsecond timestamp.  Implies -d
-T, --toggle                   toggle tracing in a process already being
                               traced. Requires -p <pid>
-u, --usecs                    toggle printing of microseconds timestamp
-V, --version                  output version information and exit
-w, --new-window               spawn program under test in a new window
```

```
    MASK can be any combination of the following mnemonics and/or hex values
    (0x is optional).  Combine masks with '+' or ',' like so:

                    --mask=wm+system,malloc+0x00800


    Mnemonic Hex       Corresponding Def  Description
    =====================================================================
    all      0x000001 (_STRACE_ALL)      All strace messages.
    flush    0x000002 (_STRACE_FLUSH)    Flush output buffer after each message.
    inherit  0x000004 (_STRACE_INHERIT)  Children inherit mask from parent.
    uhoh     0x000008 (_STRACE_UHOH)     Unusual or weird phenomenon.
    syscall  0x000010 (_STRACE_SYSCALL)  System calls.
    startup  0x000020 (_STRACE_STARTUP)  argc/envp printout at startup.
    debug    0x000040 (_STRACE_DEBUG)    Info to help debugging.
    paranoid 0x000080 (_STRACE_PARANOID) Paranoid info.
    termios  0x000100 (_STRACE_TERMIOS)  Info for debugging termios stuff.
    select   0x000200 (_STRACE_SELECT)   Info on ugly select internals.
    wm       0x000400 (_STRACE_WM)       Trace Windows msgs (enable _strace_wm).
    sigp     0x000800 (_STRACE_SIGP)     Trace signal and process handling.
    minimal  0x001000 (_STRACE_MINIMAL)  Very minimal strace output.
    pthread  0x002000 (_STRACE_PTHREAD)  Pthread calls.
    exitdump 0x004000 (_STRACE_EXITDUMP) Dump strace cache on exit.
    system   0x008000 (_STRACE_SYSTEM)   Serious error; goes to console and log.
    nomutex  0x010000 (_STRACE_NOMUTEX)  Don't use mutex for synchronization.
    malloc   0x020000 (_STRACE_MALLOC)   Trace malloc calls.
    thread   0x040000 (_STRACE_THREAD)   Thread-locking calls.
    special  0x100000 (_STRACE_SPECIAL)  Special debugging printfs for
                                         non-checked-in code
```

Description

The **strace** program executes a program, and optionally the children of the program, reporting any Cygwin DLL output from the program(s) to stdout, or to a file with the -o option. With the -w option, you can start an strace session in a new window, for example:

```
$ strace -o tracing_output -w sh -c 'while true; do echo "tracing..."; done' &
```

This is particularly useful for **strace** sessions that take a long time to complete.

Note that **strace** is a standalone Windows program and so does not rely on the Cygwin DLL itself (you can verify this with **cygcheck**). As a result it does not understand symlinks. This program is mainly useful for debugging the Cygwin DLL itself.

3.8.21 tzset

tzset — Print POSIX-compatible timezone ID from current Windows timezone setting

Synopsis

```
tzset [OPTION]
```

Options

```
Options:
  -h, --help                output usage information and exit.
  -V, --version             output version information and exit.
```

Description

Use tzset to set your TZ variable. In POSIX-compatible shells like bash, dash, mksh, or zsh:

```
export TZ=$(tzset)
```

In csh-compatible shells like tcsh:

```
setenv TZ `tzset`
```

The **tzset** tool reads the current timezone from Windows and generates a POSIX-compatible timezone information for the TZ environment variable from that information. That's all there is to it. For the way how to use it, see the above usage information.

3.8.22 umount

umount — Unmount filesystems

Synopsis

```
umount [OPTION] [<posixpath>]
```

Options

```
  -h, --help                output usage information and exit
  -U, --remove-user-mounts  remove all user mounts
  -V, --version             output version information and exit
```

Description

The **umount** program removes mounts from the mount table in the current session. If you specify a POSIX path that corresponds to a current mount point, **umount** will remove it from the current mount table. Note that you can only remove user mount points. The -U flag may be used to specify removing all user mount points from the current user session.

See Section 3.1.2 for more information on the mount table.

3.9   Using Cygwin effectively with Windows

Cygwin is not a full operating system, and so must rely on Windows for accomplishing some tasks. For example, Cygwin provides a POSIX view of the Windows filesystem, but does not provide filesystem drivers of its own. Therefore part of using Cygwin effectively is learning to use Windows effectively. Many Windows utilities provide a good way to interact with Cygwin's predominately command-line environment. For example, **ipconfig.exe** provides information about network configuration, and **net.exe** views and configures network file and printer resources. Most of these tools support the /? switch to display usage information.

Unfortunately, no standard set of tools included with all versions of Windows exists. Generally, the younger the Windows version, the more complete are the on-board tools. Microsoft also provides free downloads for Windows XP (the Windows Support Tools). Additionally, many independent sites such as download.com, simtel.net, and Microsoft's own Sysinternals provide quite useful command-line utilities, as far as they are not already provided by Cygwin. A few Windows tools, such as **find.exe**, **link.exe** and **sort.exe**, may conflict with the Cygwin versions make sure that you use the full path (**/usr/bin/find**) or that your Cygwin bin directory comes first in your PATH.

3.9.1   Pathnames

Windows programs do not understand POSIX pathnames, so any arguments that reference the filesystem must be in Windows (or DOS) format or translated. Cygwin provides the **cygpath** utility for converting between Windows and POSIX paths. A complete description of its options and examples of its usage are in cygpath(1), including a shell script for starting Windows Explorer in any directory. The same format works for most Windows programs, for example

```
notepad.exe "$(cygpath -aw "Desktop/Phone Numbers.txt")"
```

A few programs require a Windows-style, semicolon-delimited path list, which **cygpath** can translate from a POSIX path with the -p option. For example, a Java compilation from **bash** might look like this:

```
javac -cp "$(cygpath -pw "$CLASSPATH")" hello.java
```

Since using quoting and subshells is somewhat awkward, it is often preferable to use **cygpath** in shell scripts.

3.9.2   Cygwin and Windows Networking

Many popular Cygwin packages, such as ncftp, lynx, and wget, require a network connection. Since Cygwin relies on Windows for connectivity, if one of these tools is not working as expected you may need to troubleshoot using Windows tools. The first test is to see if you can reach the URL's host with **ping.exe**, one of the few utilities included with every Windows version since Windows 95. If you chose to install the inetutils package, you may have both Windows and Cygwin versions of utilities such as **ftp** and **telnet**. If you are having problems using one of these programs, see if the alternate one works as expected.

There are a variety of other programs available for specific situations. If your system does not have an always-on network connection, you may be interested in **rasdial.exe** for automating dialup connections. Users who frequently change their network configuration can script these changes with **netsh.exe**. For proxy users, the open source NTLM Authorization Proxy Server or the no-charge Hummingbird SOCKS Proxy may allow you to use Cygwin network programs in your environment.

3.9.3   The cygutils package

The optional cygutils package contains miscellaneous tools that are small enough to not require their own package. It is not included in a default Cygwin install; select it from the Utils category in **setup.exe**. Several of the cygutils tools are useful for interacting with Windows.

One of the hassles of Unix-Windows interoperability is the different line endings on text files. As mentioned in Section 3.2, Unix tools such as **tr** can convert between CRLF and LF endings, but cygutils provides several dedicated programs: **conv**, **d2u**, **dos2unix**, **u2d**, and **unix2dos**. Use the --help switch for usage information.

3.9.4   Creating shortcuts with cygutils

Another problem area is between Unix-style links, which link one file to another, and Microsoft .lnk files, which provide a shortcut to a file. They seem similar at first glance but, in reality, are fairly different. By default, Cygwin does not create symlinks as .lnk files, but there's an option to do that, see Section 3.5. These symlink .lnk files are compatible with Windows-created .lnk files, but they are still different. They do not include much of the information that is available in a standard Microsoft shortcut, such as the working directory, an icon, etc. The cygutils package includes a **mkshortcut** utility for creating standard native Microsoft .lnk files.

But here's the problem. If Cygwin handled these native shortcuts like any other symlink, you could not archive Microsoft .lnk files into **tar** archives and keep all the information in them. After unpacking, these shortcuts would have lost all the extra information and would be no different than standard Cygwin symlinks. Therefore these two types of links are treated differently. Unfortunately, this means that the usual Unix way of creating and using symlinks does not work with native Windows shortcuts.

3.9.5   Printing with cygutils

There are several options for printing from Cygwin, including the **lpr** found in cygutils (not to be confused with the native Windows **lpr.exe**). The easiest way to use cygutils' **lpr** is to specify a default device name in the PRINTER environment variable. You may also specify a device on the command line with the -d or -P options, which will override the environment variable setting.

A device name may be a UNC path (\\server_name\printer_name), a reserved DOS device name (prn, lpt1), or a local port name that is mapped to a printer share. Note that forward slashes may be used in a UNC path (//server_name/printer_name), which is helpful when using **lpr** from a shell that uses the backslash as an escape character.

lpr sends raw data to the printer; no formatting is done. Many, but not all, printers accept plain text as input. If your printer supports PostScript, packages such as a2ps and enscript can prepare text files for printing. The ghostscript package also provides some translation from PostScript to various native printer languages. Additionally, a native Windows application for printing PostScript, **gsprint**, is available from the Ghostscript website.

Chapter 4

Programming with Cygwin

4.1 Using GCC with Cygwin

4.1.1 Standard Usage

Use gcc to compile, just like under UNIX. Refer to the GCC User's Guide for information on standard usage and options. Here's a simple example:

Example 4.1 Building Hello World with GCC

```
bash$ gcc hello.c -o hello.exe
bash$ hello.exe
Hello, World

bash$
```

4.1.2 Building applications for 64 bit Cygwin

The 64 bit Cygwin toolchain uses the Microsoft x64 calling convention by default, so you can create applications using the Win32 API just as with the 32 bit Cygwin toolchain.

There's just one important difference. The 64 bit Cygwin compilers use a different data model than the Mingw and Microsoft compilers. For reference, see the Wikipedia entry on 64-bit computing.

While the Mingw and Microsoft compilers use the LLP64 data model, Cygwin compilers use the LP64 data model, just like Linux. This affects the size of the type long. In the LLP64 model preferred by Microsoft, sizeof(long) is 4. This applies for the related Win32 types like LONG, ULONG, DWORD, etc., too.

In the LP64 model used by Cygwin, sizeof(long) is 8, just like the size of pointers or the types size_t/ssize_t. This simplifies porting Linux applications to 64 bit Cygwin, but it requires due diligence when calling Windows functions taking LONG, ULONG, DWORD, or any other equivalent type. This is especially important in conjunction with pointers.

Here's an example. The Win32 function ReadFile returns the number of read bytes via a pointer to a DWORD variable:

```
BOOL WINAPI ReadFile (HANDLE, PVOID, DWORD, PDWORD, LPOVERLAPPED);
```

Note that the forth parameter is a pointer to a DWORD, thus it's a pointer to a 4 byte type, on 32 as well as on 64 bit Windows. Now we write our own my_read function using ReadFile:

Example 4.2 64bit-programming, Using ReadFile, 1st try

```
ssize_t
my_read (int fd, void *buffer, size_t bytes_to_read)
{
  HANDLE fh = _get_osfhandle (fd);
  ssize_t bytes_read;

  if (ReadFile (fh, buffer, bytes_to_read, (PDWORD) &bytes_read, NULL))
    return bytes_read;
  set_errno_from_get_last_error ();
  return -1;
}
```

While this example code works fine on 32 bit Windows, it has in fact a bad bug. The assumption that the size of ssize_t is the same as the size of DWORD is wrong for 64 bit. In fact, since `sizeof(ssize_t)` is 8, ReadFile will write the number of read bytes into the lower 4 bytes of the variable bytes_read, while the upper 4 bytes will contain an undefined value. my_read will very likely return the wrong number of read bytes to the caller.

Here's the fixed version of my_read:

Example 4.3 64bit-programming, Using ReadFile, 2nd try

```
ssize_t
my_read (int fd, void *buffer, size_t bytes_to_read)
{
  HANDLE fh = _get_osfhandle (fd);
  DWORD bytes_read;

  if (ReadFile (fh, buffer, bytes_to_read, &bytes_read, NULL))
    return (ssize_t) bytes_read;
  set_errno_from_get_last_error ();
  return -1;
}
```

4.1.3 GUI Mode Applications

Cygwin comes with an X server, so usually you should compile your GUI applications as X applications to allow better interoperability with other Cygwin GUI applications.

Other than that, Cygwin allows you to build programs with full access to the standard Windows API, including the GUI functions as defined in any Microsoft or off-the-shelf publication.

The build process is similar to any other build process. The only difference is that you use **gcc -mwindows** to link your program into a GUI application instead of a command-line application. Here's an example Makefile:

```
myapp.exe : myapp.o myapp.res
  gcc -mwindows myapp.o myapp.res -o $@

myapp.res : myapp.rc resource.h
  windres $< -O coff -o $@
```

Note the use of `windres` to compile the Windows resources into a COFF-format `.res` file. That will include all the bitmaps, icons, and other resources you need, into one handy object file. For more information on `windres`, consult the Binutils manual.

4.2 Debugging Cygwin Programs

When your program doesn't work right, it usually has a "bug" in it, meaning there's something wrong with the program itself that is causing unexpected results or crashes. Diagnosing these bugs and fixing them is made easy by special tools called *debuggers*. In the case of Cygwin, the debugger is GDB, which stands for "GNU DeBugger". This tool lets you run your program in a controlled environment where you can investigate the state of your program while it is running or after it crashes. Crashing programs sometimes create "core" files. In Cygwin these are regular text files that cannot be used directly by GDB.

Before you can debug your program, you need to prepare your program for debugging. What you need to do is add -g to all the other flags you use when compiling your sources to objects.

Example 4.4 Compiling with -g

```
bash$ gcc -g -O2 -c myapp.c
bash$ gcc -g myapp.c -o myapp
```

What this does is add extra information to the objects (they get much bigger too) that tell the debugger about line numbers, variable names, and other useful things. These extra symbols and debugging information give your program enough information about the original sources so that the debugger can make debugging much easier for you.

To invoke GDB, simply type **gdb myapp.exe** at the command prompt. It will display some text telling you about itself, then (gdb) will appear to prompt you to enter commands. Whenever you see this prompt, it means that gdb is waiting for you to type in a command, like **run** or **help**. Oh :-) type **help** to get help on the commands you can type in, or read the [?] for a complete description of GDB and how to use it.

If your program crashes and you're trying to figure out why it crashed, the best thing to do is type **run** and let your program run. After it crashes, you can type **where** to find out where it crashed, or **info locals** to see the values of all the local variables. There's also a **print** that lets you look at individual variables or what pointers point to.

If your program is doing something unexpected, you can use the **break** command to tell gdb to stop your program when it gets to a specific function or line number:

Example 4.5 "break" in gdb

```
(gdb) break my_function
(gdb) break 47
```

Now, when you type **run** your program will stop at that "breakpoint" and you can use the other gdb commands to look at the state of your program at that point, modify variables, and **step** through your program's statements one at a time.

Note that you may specify additional arguments to the **run** command to provide command-line arguments to your program. These two cases are the same as far as your program is concerned:

Example 4.6 Debugging with command line arguments

```
bash$ myprog -t foo --queue 47

bash$ gdb myprog
(gdb) run -t foo --queue 47
```

4.3 Building and Using DLLs

DLLs are Dynamic Link Libraries, which means that they're linked into your program at run time instead of build time. There are three parts to a DLL:

- the exports
- the code and data

- the import library

The code and data are the parts you write - functions, variables, etc. All these are merged together, like if you were building one big object files, and put into the dll. They are not put into your .exe at all.

The exports contains a list of functions and variables that the dll makes available to other programs. Think of this as the list of "global" symbols, the rest being hidden. Normally, you'd create this list by hand with a text editor, but it's possible to do it automatically from the list of functions in your code. The dlltool program creates the exports section of the dll from your text file of exported symbols.

The import library is a regular UNIX-like .a library, but it only contains the tiny bit of information needed to tell the OS how your program interacts with ("imports") the dll. This information is linked into your .exe. This is also generated by dlltool.

4.3.1 Building DLLs

This page gives only a few simple examples of gcc's DLL-building capabilities. To begin an exploration of the many additional options, see the gcc documentation and website, currently at http://gcc.gnu.org/

Let's go through a simple example of how to build a dll. For this example, we'll use a single file myprog.c for the program (myprog.exe) and a single file mydll.c for the contents of the dll (mydll.dll).

Fortunately, with the latest gcc and binutils the process for building a dll is now pretty simple. Say you want to build this minimal function in mydll.c:

```
#include <stdio.h>

int
hello()
{
  printf ("Hello World!\n");
}
```

First compile mydll.c to object code:

```
gcc -c mydll.c
```

Then, tell gcc that it is building a shared library:

```
gcc -shared -o mydll.dll mydll.o
```

That's it! To finish up the example, you can now link to the dll with a simple program:

```
int
main ()
{
  hello ();
}
```

Then link to your dll with a command like:

```
gcc -o myprog myprog.c -L./ -lmydll
```

However, if you are building a dll as an export library, you will probably want to use the complete syntax:

```
gcc -shared -o cyg${module}.dll \
    -Wl,--out-implib=lib${module}.dll.a \
    -Wl,--export-all-symbols \
    -Wl,--enable-auto-import \
    -Wl,--whole-archive ${old_libs} \
    -Wl,--no-whole-archive ${dependency_libs}
```

The name of your library is ${module}, prefixed with cyg for the DLL and lib for the import library. Cygwin DLLs use the cyg prefix to differentiate them from native-Windows MinGW DLLs, see the MinGW website for more details. ${old_libs} are all your object files, bundled together in static libs or single object files and the ${dependency_libs} are import libs you need to link against, e.g '-lpng -lz -L/usr/local/special -lmyspeciallib'.

4.3.2 Linking Against DLLs

If you have an existing DLL already, you need to build a Cygwin-compatible import library. If you have the source to compile the DLL, see Section 4.3.1 for details on having `gcc` build one for you. If you do not have the source or a supplied working import library, you can get most of the way by creating a .def file with these commands (you might need to do this in `bash` for the quoting to work correctly):

```
echo EXPORTS > foo.def
nm foo.dll | grep ' T _' | sed 's/.* T _//' >> foo.def
```

Note that this will only work if the DLL is not stripped. Otherwise you will get an error message: "No symbols in foo.dll".

Once you have the `.def` file, you can create an import library from it like this:

```
dlltool --def foo.def --dllname foo.dll --output-lib foo.a
```

4.4 Defining Windows Resources

`windres` reads a Windows resource file (`*.rc`) and converts it to a res or coff file. The syntax and semantics of the input file are the same as for any other resource compiler, so please refer to any publication describing the Windows resource format for details. Also, the `windres` program itself is fully documented in the Binutils manual. Here's an example of using it in a project:

```
myapp.exe : myapp.o myapp.res
  gcc -mwindows myapp.o myapp.res -o $@

myapp.res : myapp.rc resource.h
  windres $< -O coff -o $@
```

What follows is a quick-reference to the syntax `windres` supports.

```
id ACCELERATORS suboptions
BEG
"^C" 12
"Q" 12
65 12
65 12 , VIRTKEY ASCII NOINVERT SHIFT CONTROL ALT
65 12 , VIRTKEY, ASCII, NOINVERT, SHIFT, CONTROL, ALT
(12 is an acc_id)
END

SHIFT, CONTROL, ALT require VIRTKEY


id BITMAP memflags "filename"
memflags defaults to MOVEABLE


id CURSOR memflags "filename"
memflags defaults to MOVEABLE,DISCARDABLE


id DIALOG memflags exstyle x,y,width,height styles BEG controls END
id DIALOGEX memflags exstyle x,y,width,height styles BEG controls END
id DIALOGEX memflags exstyle x,y,width,height,helpid styles BEG controls END

memflags defaults to MOVEABLE
```

```
exstyle may be EXSTYLE=number
styles: CAPTION "string"
  CLASS id
  STYLE  FOO | NOT FOO | (12)
  EXSTYLE number
  FONT number, "name"
  FONT number, "name",weight,italic
  MENU id
  CHARACTERISTICS number
  LANGUAGE number,number
  VERSIONK number
controls:
  AUTO3STATE params
  AUTOCHECKBOX params
  AUTORADIOBUTTON params
  BEDIT params
  CHECKBOX params
  COMBOBOX params
  CONTROL ["name",] id, class, style, x,y,w,h [,exstyle] [data]
  CONTROL ["name",] id, class, style, x,y,w,h, exstyle, helpid [data]
  CTEXT params
  DEFPUSHBUTTON params
  EDITTEXT params
  GROUPBOX params
  HEDIT params
  ICON ["name",] id, x,y [data]
  ICON ["name",] id, x,y,w,h, style, exstyle [data]
  ICON ["name",] id, x,y,w,h, style, exstyle, helpid [data]
  IEDIT params
  LISTBOX params
  LTEXT params
  PUSHBOX params
  PUSHBUTTON params
  RADIOBUTTON params
  RTEXT params
  SCROLLBAR params
  STATE3 params
  USERBUTTON "string", id, x,y,w,h, style, exstyle
params:
  ["name",] id, x, y, w, h, [data]
  ["name",] id, x, y, w, h, style [,exstyle] [data]
  ["name",] id, x, y, w, h, style, exstyle, helpid [data]

[data] is optional BEG (string|number) [,(string|number)] (etc) END


id FONT memflags "filename"
memflags defaults to MOVEABLE|DISCARDABLE

id ICON memflags "filename"
memflags defaults to MOVEABLE|DISCARDABLE

LANGUAGE num,num

id MENU options BEG items END
items:
  "string", id, flags
  SEPARATOR
  POPUP "string" flags BEG menuitems END
flags:
  CHECKED
  GRAYED
```

```
  HELP
  INACTIVE
  MENUBARBREAK
  MENUBREAK

id MENUEX suboptions BEG items END
items:
  MENUITEM "string"
  MENUITEM "string", id
  MENUITEM "string", id, type [,state]
  POPUP "string" BEG items END
  POPUP "string", id BEG items END
  POPUP "string", id, type BEG items END
  POPUP "string", id, type, state [,helpid] BEG items END

id MESSAGETABLE memflags "filename"
memflags defaults to MOVEABLE

id RCDATA suboptions BEG (string|number) [,(string|number)] (etc) END

STRINGTABLE suboptions BEG strings END
strings:
  id "string"
  id, "string"

(User data)
id id suboptions BEG (string|number) [,(string|number)] (etc) END

id VERSIONINFO stuffs BEG verblocks END
stuffs: FILEVERSION num,num,num,num
  PRODUCTVERSION num,num,num,num
  FILEFLAGSMASK num
  FILEOS num
  FILETYPE num
  FILESUBTYPE num
verblocks:
  BLOCK "StringFileInfo" BEG BLOCK BEG vervals END END
  BLOCK "VarFileInfo" BEG BLOCK BEG vertrans END END
vervals: VALUE "foo","bar"
vertrans: VALUE num,num



suboptions:
  memflags
  CHARACTERISTICS num
  LANGUAGE num,num
  VERSIONK num

memflags are MOVEABLE/FIXED PURE/IMPURE PRELOAD/LOADONCALL DISCARDABLE
```

Made in the USA
Columbia, SC
27 April 2018